MYSTERIES, LEGENDS, AND UNEXPLAINED PHENOMENA

BIGFOOT, YETI, AND OTHER APE-MEN

MYSTERIES, LEGENDS, AND UNEXPLAINED PHENOMENA

Astrology and Divination

Bigfoot, Yeti, and Other Ape-Men

ESP, Psychokinesis, and Psychics

Ghosts and Haunted Places

Lake and Sea Monsters

Shamanism

UFOs and Aliens

Vampires

Werewolves

Witches and Wiccans

MYSTERIES, LEGENDS, AND UNEXPLAINED PHENOMENA

BIGFOOT, YETI, AND OTHER APE-MEN

PRESTON DENNETT
Consulting Editor: Rosemary Ellen Guiley

CHELSEA HOUSE
PUBLISHERS
An imprint of Infobase Publishing

BIGFOOT, YETI, AND OTHER APE-MEN

Chelsea House
An imprint of Infobase Publishing
132 West 31st Street
New York NY 10001

Library of Congress Cataloging-in-Publication Data
Dennett, Preston E., 1965-
  Bigfoot, Yeti, and other ape-men / Preston Dennett ; consulting editor, Rosemary Ellen Guiley. — 1st ed.
    p. cm. — (Mysteries, legends, and unexplained phenomena)
  Includes bibliographical references (p.   ) and index.
  ISBN-13: 978-0-7910-9386-3 (alk. paper)
  ISBN-10: 0-7910-9386-7 (alk. paper)
  1. Sasquatch. 2. Yeti. 3. Monsters. I. Guiley, Rosemary. II. Title. III. Series.

QL89.2.S2D47 2008
001.944—dc22

                           2008024229

Chelsea House books are available at special discounts when purchased in bulk quantities for businesses, associations, institutions, or sales promotions. Please call our Special Sales Department in New York at (212) 967-8800 or (800) 322-8755.

You can find Chelsea House on the World Wide Web at http://www.chelseahouse.com

Text design by James Scotto-Lavino
Cover design by Ben Peterson
Cover illustration by Robert M. Place

Printed in the United States of America

Bang EJB 10 9 8 7 6 5 4 3 2 1

This book is printed on acid-free paper.

All links and Web addresses were checked and verified to be correct at the time of publication. Because of the dynamic nature of the Web, some addresses and links may have changed since publication and may no longer be valid.

Contents

Foreword

Did you ever have an experience that turned your whole world upside down? Maybe you saw a ghost or a UFO. Perhaps you had an unusual, vivid dream that seemed real. Maybe you suddenly knew that a certain event was going to happen in the future. Or, perhaps you saw a creature or a being that did not fit the description of anything known in the natural world. At first you might have thought your imagination was playing tricks on you. Then, perhaps, you wondered about what you experienced and went looking for an explanation.

Every day and night people have experiences they can't explain. For many people these events are life changing. Their comfort zone of what they can accept as "real" is put to the test. It takes only one such experience for people to question the reality of the mysterious worlds that might exist beyond the one we live in. Perhaps you haven't encountered the unknown, but you have an intense curiosity about it. Either way, by picking up this book, you've started an adventure to explore and learn more, and you've come to the right place! The book you hold has been written by a leading expert in the paranormal—someone who understands unusual experiences and who knows the answers to your questions.

As a seeker of knowledge, you have plenty of company. Mythology, folklore, and records of the past show that human beings have had paranormal experiences throughout history. Even prehistoric cave paintings and gravesites indicate that early humans had concepts of the supernatural and of an afterlife. Humans have always sought to understand paranormal experiences and to put them into a frame of reference that makes sense to us in our daily lives. Some of the greatest minds in history have grappled with questions about the paranormal. For example, Greek philosopher Plato pondered the nature of dreams and how we "travel" during them. Isaac Newton was interested in the esoteric study of alchemy, which has magical elements, and St. Thomas Aquinas explored the nature of angels and spirits. Philosopher William James joined organizations dedicated to psychical research; and even the inventor of the light bulb, Thomas Alva Edison, wanted to build a device that could talk to the dead. More recently, physicists such as David Bohm, Stephen Hawking, William Tiller, and Michio Kaku have developed ideas that may help explain how and why paranormal phenomena happen, and neuroscience researchers like Michael Persinger have explored the nature of consciousness.

Exactly what is a paranormal experience or phenomenon? "Para" is derived from a Latin term for "beyond." So "paranormal" means "beyond normal," or things that do not fit what we experience through our five senses alone and which do not follow the laws we observe in nature and in science. Paranormal experiences and phenomena run the gamut from the awesome and marvelous, such as angels and miracles, to the downright terrifying, such as vampires and werewolves.

Paranormal experiences have been consistent throughout the ages, but explanations of them have changed as societies, cultures, and technologies have changed. For example, our ancestors were much closer to the invisible realms. In times when life was simpler, they saw, felt, and experienced other realities on a daily basis. When night fell, the darkness was thick and quiet, and it was easier to see unusual things, such as ghosts. They had no electricity to keep the night lit up. They had no media for constant communication and entertainment. Travel was difficult. They had more time to notice subtle things that were just beyond their ordinary senses. Few doubted their experiences. They accepted the invisible realms as an extension of ordinary life.

Today, we have many distractions. We are constantly busy, from the time we wake up until we go to bed. The world is full of light and noise 24 hours a day, seven days a week. We have television, the Internet, computer games, and cell phones to keep us busy, busy, busy.

We are ruled by technology and science. Yet, we still have paranormal experiences very similar to those of our ancestors. Because these occurrences do not fit neatly into science and technology, many people think they are illusions, and there are plenty of skeptics always ready to debunk the paranormal and reinforce that idea.

In roughly the past 100 years, though, some scientists have studied the paranormal and attempted to find scientific evidence for it. Psychic phenomena have proven difficult to observe and measure according to scientific standards. However, lack of scientific proof does not mean paranormal experiences do not happen. Courageous scientists are still looking for bridges between science and the supernatural.

My personal experiences are behind my lifelong study of the paranormal. Like many children I had invisible playmates when I was very young, and I saw strange lights in the yard and woods that I instinctively knew were the nature spirits who lived there. Children seem to be very open to paranormal phenomena, but their ability to have these experiences often fades away as they become more involved in the outside world, or, perhaps, as adults tell them not to believe in what they experience, that it's only in their imagination. Even when I was very young, I was puzzled that other people would tell me with great authority that I did not experience what I knew I did.

A major reason for my interest in the paranormal is precognitive dreaming experienced by members of my family. Precognition means "fore knowing," or knowing the future. My mother had a lot of psychic experiences, including dreams of future events. As a teen it seemed amazing to me that dreams could show us the future. I was determined to learn more about this and to have such dreams myself. I found books that explained extrasensory perception, the knowing of information beyond the five senses. I learned about dreams and experimented with them. I taught myself to visit distant places in my dreams and to notice details about them that I could later verify in the physical world. I learned how to send people telepathic messages in dreams and how to receive messages in dreams. Every night became an exciting adventure.

Those interests led me to other areas of the paranormal. Pretty soon I was engrossed in studying all kinds of topics. I learned different techniques for divination, including the Tarot. I learned how to meditate. I took courses to develop my own psychic skills, and I gave psychic readings to others. Everyone has at least some natural psychic ability and can improve it with attention and practice.

Next I turned my attention to the skies, to ufology, and what might be "out there" in space. I studied the lore of angels and fairies. I delved into the dark shadowy realm of demons and monsters. I learned the principles of real magic and spell casting. I undertook investigations of haunted places. I learned how to see auras and do energy healing. I even participated in some formal scientific laboratory experiments for telepathy.

My studies led me to have many kinds of experiences that have enriched my understanding of the paranormal. I cannot say that I can prove anything in scientific terms. It may be some time yet before science and the paranormal stop flirting with each other and really get together. Meanwhile, we can still learn a great deal from our personal experiences. At the very least, our paranormal experiences contribute to our inner wisdom. I encourage others to do the same as I do. Look first for natural explanations of strange phenomena. If natural explanations cannot be found or seem unlikely, consider paranormal explanations. Many paranormal experiences fall into a vague area, where although natural causes might exist, we simply don't know what could explain them. In that case I tell people to trust their intuition that they had a paranormal experience. Sometimes the explanation makes itself known later on.

I have concluded from my studies and experiences that invisible dimensions are layered upon our world, and that many paranormal experiences occur when there are openings between worlds. The doorways often open at unexpected times. You take a trip, visit a haunted place, or have a strange dream—and suddenly reality shifts. You get a glimpse behind the curtain that separates the ordinary from the extraordinary.

The books in this series will introduce you to these exciting and mysterious subjects. You'll learn many things that will astonish you. You'll be given lots of tips for how to explore the paranormal on your own. Paranormal investigation is a popular field, and you don't have to be a scientist or a full-time researcher to explore it. There are many things you can do in your free time. The knowledge you gain from these books will help prepare you for any unusual and unexpected experiences.

As you go deeper into your study of the paranormal, you may come up with new ideas for explanations. That's one of the appealing aspects of paranormal investigation—there is always room for bold ideas. So, keep an open and curious mind, and think big. Mysterious worlds are waiting for you!

—Rosemary Ellen Guiley

Introduction

Taller than a human, smellier than a skunk, and stronger than a bear, the hairy creature known as **Bigfoot**, and also called **Sasquatch**, has been reported for centuries and continues to be reported today. Bigfoot has been encountered mostly in North America and Canada. They are said to be about seven to 12 feet tall, with a small pointed head, no neck, broad chest, and long powerful arms. Their hair is usually brown, but there are reports of those with black hair, red hair, and even a few Sasquatch with white hair.

Bigfoot, however, is not the only legendary, unknown **primate**, the most highly developed order of mammals, to inhabit Earth's wilderness areas. On the other side of the world in Asia, India, and Tibet, there are reports of a similar though shorter version of the Bigfoot known as the **Yeti**. Other reports of Bigfoot and wild **ape-men** come from Russia, South America, and many other areas. In fact, reports of different types of unknown ape-men come from a wide variety of locations across the planet, each with their own unique name.

Cryptozoology (literally "hidden creatures") is the study of animals that are unknown or unacknowledged by mainstream science. Biologists estimate that more than two million different species exist in the world, and new species are discovered each year. Throughout the 1800s scientists didn't believe in the existence of panda bears, platypuses, or giant gorillas. Today, of course, there is no doubt that these animals exist. It wasn't until explorers obtained actual specimens, though, that the existence of these animals was officially accepted. The gorilla wasn't recognized as an actual species until 1849. Whether one believes in Bigfoot and the Yeti, or not, the fact is hundreds of people report encounters with them each year, and there are now literally thousands of cases on record from across the world.

There are many different ways to encounter Bigfoot or Yeti, including finding footprints (the most rare type of encounter), hearing their screams, smelling their odor, or—perhaps most common—a face-to-face encounter.

The existence of these unknown creatures has been accepted by local native populations for centuries. Native American tribes not only knew about them, but they had a long oral tradition about the creature. They believed that it was friendly unless provoked, and advised that the creature should be left alone.

Local populations in Tibet, China, and Asia have oral traditions of similar creatures, passed from generation to generation.

The modern world was first introduced to the idea of ape-men, specifically the Yeti, in the early 1900s when Himalayan explorers began to report their encounters with the creature or its footprints. It wasn't until 1920 when a climbing expedition encountered several human-like creatures that the story really exploded. This brought about numerous other expeditions that were formed specifically to find the Yeti, and which also encountered the creature. In 1951 members of an expedition in the Himalayas photographed a long set of mysterious footprints made by the alleged creature. And so the myth of the Yeti or **Abominable Snowman** became firmly established.

A few years later in the United States Bigfoot was about to make his first appearance. In 1958 a construction crew had been ordered to build a road through the forests in Bluff Creek, in northern California. Halfway through the project, the crew discovered hundreds of enormous footprints around their site. At the same time, their equipment was vandalized by what appeared to be a hugely powerful creature. The event received enormous publicity and the name Bigfoot was first introduced to the mainstream public.

In 1966 filmmaker and Bigfoot hunter Roger Patterson claimed to have encountered and filmed a female Bigfoot walking across a field and into the forest. The incredibly clear footage stunned the world.

Artist's rendering of a Bigfoot. (Kesara Art)

Bigfoot, it appeared, was real. Suddenly, the floodgates opened, and people who had been afraid to reveal their encounters now stepped forward.

Bigfoot became front-page news and the reports spread like wildfire, often coming from very credible witnesses, including police officers and park rangers. Other reports came from campers, hikers, hunters, and late-night drivers. From this point on, new cases would number in the hundreds each year. This avalanche of reports also sparked a new phenomenon: crowds of Bigfoot-hunters eager to capture one of the elusive creatures, either on film or in a cage—dead or alive.

Any mystery raises many questions. Who are these strange creatures? Are they dangerous? Are they friendly or hostile? Are they intelligent? If they are real, how have they remained hidden for so long? Where's the evidence, the proof of their existence?

This book shall examine the evidence for Bigfoot, Yeti and other mysterious ape-men. It will look around the world to various cultures to see what kind of ape-man might be lurking there. Starting with the early historical sightings and continuing to the present day, it will explore some of the most famous and controversial cases.

The journey starts deep in the heart of the frozen Himalayas in Tibet and Nepal to determine if the Yeti truly does wander the high mountain ranges. It then moves across the world to North America. Does a 12-foot-tall creature known as Sasquatch inhabit the Redwood forests of the northwestern United States? Is there really a skunk-ape prowling in the Florida Everglades? The journey across North America will include visits with these and other famous cases including Momo the Missouri Monster, Old Yellow Top of Ontario, Canada, and Old Cripple Foot of Bossburg, Washington.

From there the journey moves back across the world to examine more Yeti and ape-man reports from the Far East, looking at the Russian Sasquatch (called *Almas*) and the many accounts of Chinese wild-men. Next explored are the continent of Africa and the jungles of South America, Central America, and Mexico in search of the elusive ape-men allegedly living there. Even the island continent of Australia apparently contains a species of ape-man, which the local inhabitants

Artist's impression of the giant primate, Gigantopithecus, facing the silhouette of a human and mountain gorilla. Gigantopithecus lived between six million and 100,000 years ago and is the largest primate that ever existed. It would stand 3 meters tall if upright and weigh up to 500 kilograms, three times larger than modern-day gorillas. (Christian Darkin/Photo Researchers, Inc.)

call Yowies. No corner of the world will be left unexplored in the search for unknown primates.

The scientific evidence for ape-men is surprisingly extensive and includes multiple eyewitness testimonies, footprints, body prints, hair samples, dung samples, blood samples, photographs, moving films, audio recordings, and more. This book will look at the work of some of the world's Bigfoot scientists and hunters as they conduct live field investigations, and cutting-edge scientific analysis into the physical evidence. It will also examine the skeptical viewpoint, weeding out hoaxes, and looking for alternative explanations. For example, perhaps Bigfoot is really just a **Gigantopithecus**, a type of giant primate believed to be extinct. Finally we will also examine some of the most controversial and unusual cases, including kidnappings and other hostile behavior, friendly Bigfoot rescues, and even cases involving a psychic and/or UFO connection.

Are Bigfoot, Yeti, and other ape-men real? According to zoologist and leading Bigfoot researcher Ivan T. Sanderson, there could be at least four different species of these creatures. Many experts believe there are more than that. Certainly there is evidence that *something* is out there, but as of today the mystery remains unsolved.

The First Yeti

It was 1887, and Major Lawrence Waddell and a group of porters hiked through the eastern Himalayas in Tibet. As they tromped through the deep snows, they were surprised to come upon a set of large footprints that appeared to have been made by a creature with bare feet that walked upright on two legs. The tracks went off into the distance over some of the harshest terrain in the area. Waddell and the others were impressed. It seemed impossible that any human being could have made the tracks.

Waddell wrote about his encounter in his book, *Among the Himalayas*. It was apparently the first Yeti case to be recorded in the English language. His report was unique and was therefore ignored.

While the local people continued to have encounters, no scientists were willing to look into the reports. One of the first scientists to study ape-men reports was a young Russian zoologist named Vladimir Khakhlov. In the early 1900s numerous reports came of a strange creature haunting the wild areas of Eurasia. Khakhlov conducted an extensive survey of the cases, which he submitted to the Imperial Academy of Sciences in Russia. Again, nobody seemed to notice.

Another early Himalayan Yeti encounter by highly respected botanist and explorer Henry J. Elwes also failed to generate any scientific attention. In 1915 Elwes published a report of his own ape-man sighting and the sightings of others in the scientific journal *Proceedings of the Zoological Society of London*. In his report Elwes wrote,

"I have discovered the existence of another animal but cannot make out what it is, a big monkey or ape perhaps." Elwes described the creature in detail and then wrote, "It is a thing that practically no Englishman has ever heard of, but all the natives of the higher villages know about it."

It wasn't until 1921 that a Yeti encounter would finally receive the publicity it deserved. Again, it came from the Himalayas. In that year Lieutenant Colonel C. K. Howard-Bury had joined a mountain climbing expedition on Mount Everest in Tibet. He and his group were at about 17,000 feet near the Lhapka-La pass when they saw a number of dark figures traversing a snowfield far above them. They observed the figures through binoculars and saw that they were human-like but covered with dark hair. The expedition climbed up to the location. It

Figure 1.1 *An anonymous photographer took this intriguing photograph of an alleged Yeti or Sasquatch walking through the forest.* (VEER Antonia Barbagallo/ Getty Images)

The Many Names of Bigfoot

What is Bigfoot's real name? The four most common names for these unknown, hairy ape-men are Bigfoot, Sasquatch, the Yeti, and the Abominable Snowman. The truth is that there are literally hundreds of different names for these creatures. Because Bigfoot sightings are so widespread, many cultures have given the creature a unique name. For example, Native Americans have more than 100 names for the creature, the majority of which translate into some variation of "wild-man of the woods." What follows is only a partial list of some of the many names of Bigfoot and the Yeti based on their region.

Africa: *Kikomba, Tano Giant, Muhalu, Ufiti*

Asia: *Almas, Adam-Ja-Paiysy, Albast, Alboosty, Golbo, Golub-yavan, Guli-biavan, Kul-bii-aban, Uli-bieban, Yavan-adam, Hun-Guressu, Kun-goroos, Kumchin-gorgosu, Jelmoguz-Jez-Tyrmak, Kaptar, Ksy-Giik*

Australia: *the Yahoo, Yowie*

Borneo: *Batutut*

China: *Hun-Guresu, Yuran*

Finland: *Tree-Eater*

Japan: *Higapon*

North America: *Oh-Mah, Toki-Mussi, Hoquiam, Sayatkah, Sosskwatl, Sasquatch, Bigfoot, Arulataq, Skanicum, Stick Indian, Crazy Bear, Choanito, Night People, Scwe-ney-tum, S'cwene'y'ti, Seeahtik, Seeahtkch, Sehlatiks, Salatiks, Seatco, See'atco, Saskehavas, Skunk-Ape, Kauget, Xi'lgo, Yi'dyi'tay, At'at'ahila, Qah-line-me, Fouke Monster, Momo, Skookum, Te smai'etl Soqwaia'm, Hoquiam, S'oq'wiam, See-ah-tik, See-oh-mah, Toki-mussi, Chiye-tanka, Rugaru, Sokqueatl*

(continues)

(continued)

Philippines: *Orang-Gugu*

Scotland: *Big Gray Man*

South America: *Didi, Deedee, Dru-di-di, Didi-aguiri, Duendi*

Tibet: *Metoh-Kangmi, Dzu-Teh, the Yeti, the Abominable Snowman, Chutey, Mi-Ge, Mi-Go, Mi-Gu, Mi-Teh, Nyalmo, Rackshi-Bompo, Ri-Mi, Sogpa, Teh-lma, Zerleg-Khoon*

took several hours to reach the area, and by that time the figures were gone. However, they did find large numbers of footprints, which Colonel Howard-Bury said were "three times those of normal humans."

The Colonel speculated that the tracks were of a strange kind of creature, perhaps a wolf. However, the native Sherpas strongly disagreed and said that the tracks were made by a creature they called *Metoh-Kangmi* or "snow creature." They said that the creature was a human-like ape-man that lived at high altitudes.

Colonel Howard-Bury probably didn't realize that he would start a media frenzy when he telegraphed a report of the incident to his representatives in India. He mistranslated the name of the creature, calling it "the Abominable Snowman." Newspaper reporters heard about the incident and began to investigate. To their surprise, the creature was already known among the local population and they were even able to locate several other firsthand reports, which they published along with Howard-Bury's account.

The story of the Abominable Snowman was out. It electrified the media and was front-page news across the planet for several months. After the furor died down, the main result was that zoologists continued to debate the existence of the creature, while numerous explorers traveled from across the world to hunt for the mysterious Yeti. Since then, dozens of expeditions have been launched into the Himalayas and Mount Everest with hopes of encountering the creature. In several cases, explorers claimed to have come upon their tracks, found

(continues on page 24)

Figure 1.2 *In 1951 British explorer Eric Shipton took this photograph of an alleged Yeti footprint on the slopes of Mount Everest.* (Topical Press Agency/Getty Images)

Bigfoot & Yeti Statistics

While conclusive proof of the existence of unknown primates remains elusive, several thousand recorded reports now make it possible to construct a fairly accurate description of the alleged creatures and their behavior.

Description:

Covered with hair (usually about three to five inches long). Has very broad shoulders, muscular arms that reach down almost to the knees, a cone-shaped head, a human-like face with no visible neck. Walks on two legs, like a person, and has been reported to reach running speeds in excess of 35 miles per hour. An estimated 15 to 25 percent of the cases involve creatures that emit a powerful offensive odor. The Yeti and other ape-men are also described as being very muscular and covered with hair. Like the Bigfoot, they are bipedal and appear to have the characteristics of both an ape and a human being.

Height:

Full grown, height ranges from about six to 12 feet. The Yeti are shorter and are usually described as reaching average human height.

Weight:

Nobody has ever been able to weigh a Bigfoot, so any figures are purely estimates. Most researchers, however, believe that a full-grown specimen ranges from 500 to 1,000 pounds or more. Yeti are considerably smaller and are estimated to weigh anywhere from 150 to 300 pounds.

Footprints:

Bigfoot's most famous features are the gigantic footprints it leaves behind. These mysterious footprints range in size from about 12 to 22 inches long and 5 to 8 inches wide. Yeti footprints are somewhat smaller, ranging from about 6 to 15 inches in length and 4 to 6 inches wide.

Behavior:

Both Bigfoot and Yeti are usually very elusive, though some cases show that if provoked, the creatures become confrontational. They appear to be solitary creatures and are rarely seen in groups. Many cases exist in which Sasquatch have thrown stones at witnesses. A few cases involve hostile behavior such as chasing after witnesses, and in rare cases, kidnapping someone. They are also reported to bang on trees with sticks or crack off the tops of saplings. They are believed to be nocturnal, and when moving, they travel in dense forests, along ridge-tops, and in creek-beds. Some researchers believe that the Sasquatch purposefully avoid leaving tracks. Their level of intelligence remains unknown.

Vocalizations:

The Sasquatch and the Yeti are reported to make a wide variety of sounds. These **vocalizations** include growls, roars, high-pitched screams, hooting noises, and even whistling. In a few very rare cases, witnesses have even reported what sounds like primitive speech.

Habitat:

More than 23,000 locations in the United States are named after a Native American name for Bigfoot, and as the reports show, these mysterious creatures are widespread. However, the Pacific Northwestern United States and Canada (including California, Oregon, Washington, Idaho, and western Canada) is the number one place in the world to view a Bigfoot. The best place to view a Yeti is the foothills and high valleys of the Himalayas located in Tibet, Nepal, Russia, and China.

(continues)

(continued)

Population:

Researchers are unsure of the number of living Sasquatch and estimates vary widely. Writes Grover Krantz, "If the Sasquatch is actually as widespread over the continent as current reports would have it, we could easily postulate that there are anywhere from ten to twenty thousand of them."

(continued from page 21)

cairns of stones moved by them, heard their screams, or had face-to-face encounters with the creatures.

In 1923 members of an Everest expedition were climbing at an elevation of 17,000 feet when they observed a "great hairy, naked man running across a snowfield below."

In 1951 English explorer Eric Shipton came upon a long set of 13-inch-long tracks along the middle slopes of Mount Everest. Shipton was amazed by the tracks as they crossed over very harsh landscape. As he writes, "Where the tracks crossed a crevasse, one could see quite clearly where the creature had jumped and used its toes to secure purchase on the other side."

Other explorers had encountered similar tracks. However, unlike them, Shipton had brought a camera and took several clear photographs of the tracks. He had encountered Yeti tracks several years earlier, and this time, he was prepared. The photographs were published in the *Illustrated London News* and seemed to prove that some type of unknown primate did in fact exist in the upper reaches of the Himalayas.

Shipton's photographs ignited an uproar among mainstream scientists, some who claimed that it was either a case of hoaxing or mistaken identity. Others, however, began to wonder if the Yeti might, in fact, be real. This inspired another batch of Yeti expeditions, many of which claimed success in their search for the enigmatic ape-men.

In 1955 an Argentine mountaineering expedition and another group of English mountain climbers each reported having encountered tracks. More expeditions soon followed. By this time, the Yeti had become a permanent part of the public consciousness, and numerous other encounters would be reported each year from this point on. Still, most people assumed that the strange ape-men were limited to the high mountain ranges of Asia. On the other side of the world, though, reports of a 10-foot-tall, smelly, hairy creature were beginning to trickle into the mainstream press.[1]

The Arrival of Bigfoot

It was April 1840, and missionary Elkanah Walker sat down and began to write a letter to Reverend David Green. Walker had lived with the Spokane Indians in Washington Territory (what is now Washington State) as a missionary for several months, but because of ill health, he was writing to Reverend Green to announce that he would be resigning. In the letter, however, Green revealed that the local Nez Perces Indians believed that a "race of giants" lived in the nearby mountains. He described the creatures in detail, saying that they "frequently come in the night and steal their salmon from their nets and eat them raw. If people are awake they always know when they are coming by their strong smell, which is most intolerable. It is not uncommon for them to come in the night and give three whistles and then the stones will begin to hit their houses. The people believe that they are still troubled by their nocturnal visits."

Green's letter remains one of the earliest written records of Sasquatch. Many of the details of modern Bigfoot are present, including the bad odor, the stone-throwing behavior, and the whistling sounds, which researchers call vocalizations.

The existence of Bigfoot has been accepted as fact by numerous Native American tribes across North America for centuries. Although their encounters with the creature were not written down, oral traditions passed from generation to generation tell of a large, hairy creature that lives in the deep forests and high mountain valleys. The many different tribes were in general agreement that the Sasquatch should be left alone. They warn that the Sasquatch can become hostile if provoked or approached too closely. They may throw stones, charge, or even attack. Many of the tribes attribute magical powers to the creatures, such as invisibility or the ability to read minds. Others believe that encountering a Sasquatch is an omen of bad luck. They also believe them to be intelligent, and that they have lived among humans since the dawn of time. The first written and recorded encounters, however, emerged in the nineteenth century.

In 1886 Jack Dover was hunting in the wilds outside of Happy Camp, California when he saw a seven-foot-tall figure with a "bull dog head, short ears and long hair." The creature stood 150 yards away and was picking berries and tender shoots from bushes. When it realized it was being observed, the creature emitted a long shrill scream "like that of a woman in great fear." Dover aimed his gun and prepared to shoot but decided not to do so because the creature looked so human. After several moments the creature left.

Later Dover learned that numerous other people in the area had also seen the creature, which was believed to live in the caves of nearby Marble Mountain.[1]

BIGFOOT ON MOUNT RAINIER

Major S. E. Ingraham was a towering figure in the history of Mount Rainier in Washington State. He was a pioneering explorer of the mountain, and many geological features were named after him. He wrote several books about Mount Rainier. Then in 1895, he stunned everyone when he published a story called "The Old Man of the Mountain," which presented his true-life encounter with a Bigfoot on the summit of Mount Rainier.

Ingraham, with two companions, had reached the summit of the mountain, where they spent the night. In the middle of the night he woke up and crept inside a cave near the summit. Inside the cave, Ingraham was shocked to see a large, very strong, human-like figure covered with hair approach him. The creature stood within a few feet. Suddenly, Ingraham claims, the Bigfoot began to communicate with him telepathically. Writes Ingraham, "For an hour I received impressions from the Old Man of the Crater. It is a strange story I got from him . . . The old man told me of his abode in the interior, of another race to which he belonged and the traditions of that race. . . . This is no myth."

Ingraham reports that the creature tried to take him back into the cave, but Ingraham broke the spell and escaped back to the surface.[2]

MORE EARLY CASES

Many of the early cases come from the western coast of North America. In 1901 lumberman Mike King planned to travel to Vancouver Island in Canada to scout out possible forest wood to harvest. He often hired local Native Americans as guides, but on this occasion, he could not find a single guide who would agree to go to the area. Each of them refused, saying that a "wild-man of the woods" lived there. Mr. King decided to go alone. He hiked into the area and as he suspected, the forests were very thick. A few days into his expedition, he had an amazing encounter. Coming upon a creek, he saw a man-like creature covered with red-brown hair squatting by the shore, washing some roots and arranging them in two neat piles. The creature was very large and had unusually long arms. Suddenly, the creature stood up and ran off into the forest. King inspected the ground and found large footprints that looked like a "human foot but with phenomenally long and spreading toes."

Apparently the local natives were correct about Vancouver Island. In 1904, four hunters in the area encountered what appeared to be an adolescent Bigfoot, which was also described as having long hair on its head and a beard, both details rarely reported among Sasquatch. The creature quickly ran away before the hunters could react.

In 1907 a group of Bigfoot terrorized an entire village of Native Americans in Bishops Cove, British Columbia, Canada. The

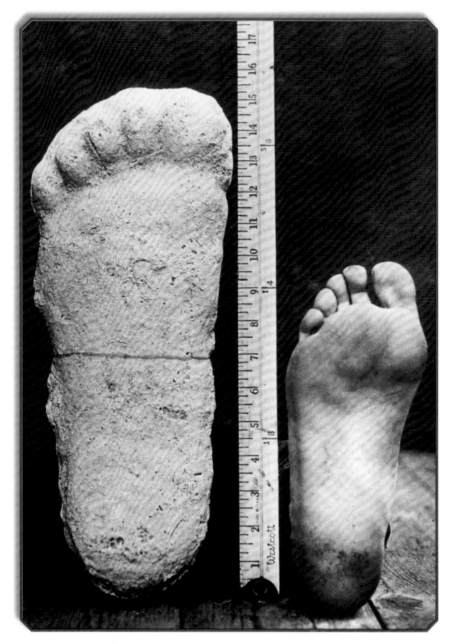

Figure 2.1 *Cast of a Bigfoot print compared to a human foot.* (Fortean Picture Library)

inhabitants claimed that several of the creatures prowled the beach at night, making extremely high-pitched screams and walking through the village. When a ship happened to dock at the area, the entire village population surrounded the ship, begging to be taken aboard and away from the area.

British Columbia soon produced several more reports, including one involving the apparent discovery of a Bigfoot's home. Sometime around 1910, a group of men were picking berries in the wilderness when they came upon a large cave. They were surprised because they had lived in the area for years and never noticed the cave before. Inside they found "a sort of stone house or enclosure." They were unable to examine further because it was too dark in the back of the cave. Says one of the witnesses, Charley Victor, "We left, intending to return in a couple of days and go on exploring. Old Indians, to whom we told the story of our discovery, warned us not to venture near the cave again, as it was surely occupied by a Sasquatch. That was the first time I heard about the hairy men that inhabit the mountains. We, however, disregarded the advice of the old men and sneaked off to explore the cave, but to our great disappointment found the boulder rolled back into the mouth and fitting over it so nicely that you might suppose it had been made for that purpose."

Another early case occurred in 1915, again in British Columbia. Frontiersmen Donald McRae, Green Hicks, and Charles Flood were hiking through the Holy Cross Mountains checking their fur traps. Hicks warned the other two men that he had encountered "wild-men" in the area before, and to be on the lookout for them. As they approached an area known as Cougar Lake, they observed an eight-foot-tall, light brown Bigfoot picking berries with one hand and eating them with the other. McRae thought it had to be a strange type of bear. Hicks argued and told him again that it was a wild-man. Flood, however, was most impressed by its mixture of human and animal features, and is convinced that it was an actual Bigfoot. He later signed a sworn statement attesting to the truth of his case.[3]

AGGRESSIVE BIGFOOT

In 1924 a group of loggers came into the town of Kelso, Washington, with an incredible story. They had just returned from their logging camp in the Cascade Mountains. They said that they had been forced to flee when a group of "enormous hairy wild-men" attacked their camp, pelting them with large stones and chasing them out of the area. Because the loggers were known to be strong and brave, a

President Theodore Roosevelt Believed in Bigfoot

Unknown to many people, former president of the United States Theodore Roosevelt not only believed in Bigfoot, he actually wrote a firsthand account about a Bigfoot encounter. In 1891 Roosevelt traveled through Yellowstone Park and heard several accounts of Bigfoot sightings, including one told to him by an old frontiersman named Bauman. Roosevelt was apparently impressed with the story as he published Bauman's story in his 1893 book titled *The Wilderness Hunter*.

Roosevelt's story describes how Bauman and his partner were camping in the mountains. The two men left their camp for a short time and upon returning discovered that some type of creature had ravaged it. At first they thought it was a bear, until they examined the footprints.

Writes Roosevelt, "The footprints of the beast were quite plain, but at first they paid no particular heed to them, busying themselves with rebuilding the lean-to, laying out their beds and stores and lighting the fire. While Bauman was making ready supper, it being already dark, his companion began to examine the tracks more closely, and soon took a brand from the fire to follow them up, where the intruder had walked along a game trail after leaving the camp.... Coming back to the fire, he stood by it a minute or two, peering out into the darkness and suddenly remarked: 'Bauman, that bear has been walking on two legs.'"

Roosevelt wrote that the two men then discussed the footprints, and both agreed that they were neither bear nor human. That night, the large posse of men was organized to return to the area and investigate. Upon arriving at the camp, the group found that their cabin had been completely destroyed by the creatures. Although the creatures were now gone, their large footprints could be seen all around the area. The loggers refused to remain and the work site was shut down.

The same year as the above encounter, a group of prospectors were working a mine in Ape Canyon on the east side of Mount St. Helens

creature returned. Bauman was awakened by a noise. He immediately smelled a terrible odor and saw the shadow of "a great body in the darkness at the mouth of the lean-to." He grabbed his rifle and shot at the creature, which immediately ran away.

In the morning the two trappers discovered that their camping gear had again been vandalized by the creature. Again, the men were puzzled, because as Roosevelt writes, "Whatever the thing was, it had walked off on but two legs."

The next night the two trappers made a roaring fire. Not surprisingly the Bigfoot returned, roaring around the camp, but never approaching too close to the fire

At this point the story turns deadly. Roosevelt writes that the next day, the two trappers became separated as they checked their traps, finding each one empty. When Bauman later returned to camp looking for his companion, he came upon a grisly site. His companion had been killed, his neck apparently broken by the creature. Writes Roosevelt, "Bauman, utterly unnerved, and believing that the creature with which he had to deal was something either half human or half devil, some great goblin-beast, abandoned everything but his rifle and struck off at great speed."

Roosevelt's story is unique in that is the one of very few reported accounts of Bigfoot actually killing a human, that is assuming the story is true. While some Bigfoot cases are hostile, these types of cases are extremely rare. Besides Roosevelt, no other presidents have ever reported any other kind of Bigfoot encounter.

in Washington State. During their stay, Fred Beck and several of the other prospectors noticed giant footprints around their cabin. This happened on several occasions, until one day, one of the miners saw a large "ape-like creature" watching them from behind a tree. He quickly fired at it with his shotgun. The creature jerked as if it had been struck and ran off into the forest. Shortly later, Fred Beck spotted another creature standing at the edge of a cliff. He shot it in the back. It fell off the cliff and was lost to view.

That night, as the miners slept in their cabin, the creatures attacked. They pounded on the cabin walls, beating at it, tearing away planks of wood and beating the walls with large rocks. This went on for five hours. As dawn approached, the creatures finally left. When the miners ventured outside, they discovered that while their cabin was still standing, the outside of it showed considerable damage. There were also hundreds of footprints surrounding the structure. Beck and the other miners decided unanimously to abandon the mine and return to civilization.

Usually Bigfoot is shy and runs away from humans. However, in some cases they display aggressive behavior. Another such case occurred in 1941 to the Chapman family who lived in Ruby Creek, British Columbia, Canada, only a few miles north of the United States' border. One bright summer afternoon, Jeannie Chapman heard her three children (ages nine, seven, and five) screaming from outside. Running outside, she saw a strange creature approaching. It was seven and a half feet tall and covered with yellow-brown hair about four inches long. The Bigfoot stared directly at Mrs. Chapman and continued to march toward the house, making loud whistling and screeching noises. The children began to panic, so she quickly gathered them together. They fled the house in a group, and ran several miles down the road back to Ruby Creek Village.

Meanwhile, the Bigfoot apparently ransacked the interior of the house. George Chapman returned later that evening and found that the Bigfoot had taken a 55-gallon barrel of salt fish and scattered its contents outside.

Figure 2.2   *Photo of an alleged Bigfoot. Many Bigfoot researchers doubt its authenticity.* (Bettmann/Corbis)

The family returned home reluctantly. Over the next week the Sasquatch returned every night, driving their dogs crazy and badly scaring them all. Each morning they found hundreds of giant footprints around the house. Although the Bigfoot hadn't entered the house, Jeannie Chapman was afraid that it was after the children. The Chapmans finally had enough and they moved out.[4]

At this point in history, Bigfoot encounters were occurring regularly, and yet they received almost no publicity. Other than the local inhabitants, very few people knew about the possible existence of these creatures. Soon an event in northern California would cause the entire world to take notice. Bigfoot was about to become front-page news.

The Classic Cases

It was August 3, 1958, and Wilbur Wallace was angry. He was the foreman of a road crew whose job it was to build a road through the thickly forested mountains outside of Bluff Creek in northern California. As Wallace inspected the work site that morning he was shocked to see that it had been vandalized. Somebody had thrown a 700-pound tire away from the work site. A nearly full 55-gallon drum of diesel fuel was also missing. Wallace saw several large tracks around the area where it had been. He finally found the oil drum at the bottom of a steep hill 175 feet away. The vandalism was bad enough, but Wallace couldn't understand who or what could be strong enough to cause this kind of damage.

A few weeks later worker Jerry Crew returned to the construction site for an inspection. He walked up to a tractor and received an incredible shock. All over the ground were hundreds of footprints. The problem was the footprints were made by somebody barefoot, and each of the prints was about 17 inches long. Just a few weeks earlier, other work crews had claimed to encounter similar footprints, though Crew had been skeptical. Now he wondered if somebody was playing some kind of joke.

Intrigued, he followed the tracks and was shocked to see that they cut straight through the forest, often traveling up and down steep inclines. The stride between the steps averaged about 50 inches, twice the length of a human stride. Crew showed the tracks to his employees, all of whom were mystified.

Over the next few weeks the mysterious track-maker returned several times. Starting on October 2, 1958, the tracks appeared three days in a row. Crew decided to make plaster casts of them to show other people.

News of the strange footprints spread through the local population. At some point a wife of one of the crewmen leaked the story to Bluff Creek newspaper journalist Andrew Genzoli, who began an investigation. Genzoli was shocked by the plaster casts of the huge footprints. After talking with Jerry Crew, he wrote a short article with photographs of the plaster casts, which was published in the *Humboldt Times.*

Around this time numerous witnesses in the area stepped forward and revealed that they had seen the Bigfoot. Ray Kerr and Bob

Figure 3.1 *Close-up of a Bigfoot footprint found in Bluff Creek, California, in 1967.* (Fortean Picture Library)

Breazele, two other men, said they saw the creature while driving at night in late October. It took the Bigfoot only two strides to cross the road. In the spring of 1959, a couple flew in their private plane over the area, following a set of tracks. At the end of the tracks they saw a Sasquatch, which they estimated at 10 feet tall. Researcher Ivan T. Sanderson attempted to locate and interview the anonymous couple, but was unsuccessful.

The result of Genzoli's article was explosive. The story became front-page news and was reprinted in newspapers across the United States and the world. Requests for information flooded to Genzoli, while reporters hounded Wallace, Crew, and others for more details.

Although Bigfoot encounters had been occurring for at least a hundred years, the large number of witnesses and the footprints made this case unique. The story electrified the world, and Bigfoot became hugely popular.

Dr. Maurice Tripp, a geologist and geophysicist from San Jose, California, studied the Bluff Creek prints and the soil in which they were made. He concluded that the creature that made the prints weighed at least 800 pounds. He was convinced the tracks were genuine. They were too large to be human, and had a step length nearly twice that of humans. But he was mostly convinced because the area where the footprints were found was very remote and rough terrain, a very unlikely location for a hoax. As he said, "It would be particularly difficult to fraudulently prepare hundreds of such tracks overnight–particularly in the type of country in which they were found."[1]

The Bluff Creek encounter was a watershed event. Before 1958 Bigfoot was virtually unknown. There were no studies about the creature, no books written on the subject, and no organizations devoted to collecting reports. Afterward, however, there was a flood of researchers, books, and hundreds of new reports. The reports came in from across the United States at a minimum of a dozen per year and often numbered up to 50 or more. Most of these involved very brief encounters.

Up to this time nobody had obtained any convincing photographs or film of the alleged creature. However, on October 18, 1967, that all changed when amateur filmmaker Roger Patterson obtained some remarkable footage of an apparent Bigfoot in Bluff Creek, California. The film was shocking. Overnight it became the single most famous and controversial case in Bigfoot history.

CAUGHT ON FILM

In early October Roger Patterson and his associate Robert Gimlin decided to start filming for a documentary film that they were producing about Bigfoot. Patterson, a professional rodeo rider, had been researching Bigfoot for nearly a decade. Because Bluff Creek was a known hotspot, the filmmakers concentrated their search there.

At first they had little luck. Then they heard about a new set of footprints that had been found in the region. On October 18, 1967, Patterson and Gimlin rode their horses through the area, occasionally taking film footage of the surroundings to use as background material for their film.

Early in the afternoon they came around a corner on the trail. Patterson noticed it first, a tall, hairy figure standing a little more than 100 feet away. At the same time his horse reared, hurling him to the ground. Patterson jumped up and quickly pulled his movie camera out of the saddlebag. By the time he turned it on and aimed it the creature was already walking away into the forest. Nevertheless, Patterson still managed to film 952 frames of moving film, 60 seconds of film, less than 20 of which showed the actual creature.

Both Gimlin and Patterson were amazed. They ran to where the creature had disappeared and found a clear set of footprints, each about 14½ inches long and 5 inches wide. They followed the tracks into the forest for three miles before the undergrowth became too thick to continue. Excited about the film, they decided to return and have it developed.

Figure 3.2   *In 1967 rodeo-rider Roger Patterson filmed what he believed to be a female Bigfoot in Bluff Creek, California. This photo taken from the film shows the alleged Bigfoot glancing toward the camera before it disappears into the forest.* (Fortean Picture Library)

Patterson wasn't sure he had gotten any clear footage, but to his delight, the film showed the creature in vivid detail. It depicted what appears to be a female Bigfoot, about seven feet tall, walking with very large strides into the forest. At one point it turns and looks at the camera, and then disappears into the trees.

Neither Patterson nor Gimlin could have predicted what happened next. As news of their sighting and the film began to spread, researchers converged on the scene. Pioneering Bigfoot investigator Bob Titmus located the tracks made by the female Bigfoot and made several plaster casts.

At the same time Patterson and Gimlin found themselves the center of media attention. In November 1967 the film was aired to media representatives in Vancouver and scientists from the University of British Columbia and the British Columbia museum. From that moment researchers and scientists became divided concerning the film's authenticity.

Skeptics said that the figure was clearly just a large man in a gorilla suit. Some even said they could see a line down the center of the back, which could be a zipper. Makeup artist John Chambers, who designed the costumes for *The Planet of the Apes* (1968), was accused of having constructed the Bigfoot suit. Chambers vehemently denied it, saying he had nothing to do with the film, which he found very convincing and way beyond his own abilities to fake. Despite this, accusations that the film was a hoax continued. More recently, a man named Bob Heironimus claimed that he actually wore the suit and participated in the hoax. Heironimus, however, has been unable to produce the gorilla suit he says he wore or any other evidence of his claims. While Bob Gimlin admitted that it was possible that the event was a hoax he was not involved in planning, he has made it clear in numerous interviews that he believed the event was not faked.

Eventually the film was analyzed in detail. Believers pointed out many indications that the film was genuine. One fact overlooked by many was that the creature never locked its knees while walking.

Human beings fully extend their legs and lock their knees straight with each step. The figure in the film, however, kept its knees bent at all times, a feature that is consistent with other Bigfoot reports.

Figure 3.3 *A set of tracks supposedly made by a Bigfoot, filmed by Roger Patterson in 1967.* (Fortean Picture Library)

Another seemingly authentic detail was that the large calf muscles in the legs could clearly be seen bulging with each step, something that would be very difficult to fake.

Finally there were the many footprints found at the scene that nobody has been able to disprove. Ultimately, experts agree that the

What Does Bigfoot Smell Like?

Primates are known to be very smelly creatures, but in the case of the Bigfoot, this odor seems to be particularly powerful. Researchers aren't exactly sure what is responsible for Bigfoot's smell, but they do have theories. Grover Krantz writes, "Some possible explanations for the rank smell are scent glands, carrion eating, and unclean personal habits."

Interestingly, there are many reports of Bigfoot not smelling bad. In fact, fewer than 25 percent of the cases involve any noticeable odor. Some researchers feel that, like the skunk, the Bigfoot may use scent glands as a defense against other creatures, including humans. Krantz says, "If this is a generated scent, at least in part, it would help to explain why the smell is noted by only some observers. The scent may be exuded at will, or automatically in response to particular circumstances."

Whatever this smell is, witnesses are often at a loss to describe it. What follows are some of the more vivid descriptions of the smell of a Sasquatch:

"I smelled a very strange odor, almost nauseating, as if something had died."

—from a 1968 encounter in Tennessee

"The first thing I noticed was the smell. It was terrible. If you ever had your dog roll in something dead, that's exactly the smell–the type that sticks in your nostrils."

—from a 1970 encounter in Oregon

footage is interesting and compelling, but it falls short of being definitive proof of Bigfoot.

Since this time, many other people have taken photographs or even moving films of Bigfoot. None of them are comparable to the close-up, vivid footage taken by Roger Patterson.

"Suddenly, I became aware of a strong offensive odor–very powerful, a combination of rotten eggs, rotten meat and sulfur, but really impossible to explain. Once smelled, though, it is never forgotten."

—from a 1972 encounter in Washington

"We noticed an odor that smelled like old roadkill mixed with cabbage."

—from a 1976 encounter in Michigan

"The thing had an awful, sour smell, something like dead meat that had set out for three or four days."

—from a 1981 encounter in Wisconsin

"[The smell was] a mixture of rotten eggs, spoiled potatoes and urine."

—from a 1982 encounter in Pennsylvania

"My sighting began with a bad smell. It smelled worse than a dog that had been playing in the sewer."

—from a 1982 encounter in Kentucky

"Then the smell came. It was foul garbage, garlic, skunk and human body odor all rolled into one."

—from a 1997 encounter in Connecticut

"He smells like dirty feet and stinky tennis shoes and rotting dead animal. He smells like a dumpster at high noon. It's really an odd smell. It smells like feces and manure and rotting flesh."

—from a 1998 encounter in California

Both Patterson and Gimlin stuck to their story. Despite the many accusations of hoaxes, nobody has ever been able to prove the film a hoax, or produce the gorilla-suit that was allegedly used to make it. Gimlin seemed embarrassed by all the media attention and remained largely private. He is currently in his seventies and lives in Yakima, Washington. Roger Patterson, however, embraced the media and showed his film around the world. He finished and released his documentary entitled *America's Abominable Snowman*. He died in January 1972, only four years after shooting the most famous Bigfoot film in history.[2]

OLD CRIPPLE FOOT

In October 1969 Joe Rhodes, a butcher, was shocked to find a clear set of giant footprints while hiking in the wilderness outside of Bossburg in Washington State, where he lived. A few local residents reported seeing a Bigfoot feeding out of roadside garbage cans around the same time. Rhodes alerted local Bigfoot researcher Ivan Marx, who made plaster casts of the prints. Marx then called in Bigfoot expert René Dahinden. Together they explored the area and were amazed to come upon additional tracks. They followed them for more than a half-mile. Dahinden counted more than 1,089 actual footprints. The tracks led out of and back into a reservoir, crossing over a barbed wire fence. Each of the prints was 17 inches long.

Researchers who studied the prints were impressed by their apparent authenticity. Most interesting was that the tracks made by the right foot of the creature were all distorted in exactly the same way, showing that the Bigfoot suffered from some sort of disease or injury to the right foot. Researchers quickly dubbed the Sasquatch "Old Cripple Foot." The right footprints all curved inward, were missing the smallest toe, and had two large bulges on the outer edge. For researcher Grover Krantz, the footprints provided "the first convincing evidence that the animals were real."

Krantz personally investigated the footprints and found further evidence that left him totally convinced. Writes Krantz, "I was able to

Figure 3.4 *This late-1960s photo shows Roger Patterson (right) and Rene Dahinden (left) displaying plaster casts of footprints found at Bluff Creek in northern California in 1964.* (Fortean Picture Library)

locate a well-built fence that had been crossed by the line of footprints with scarcely a break in stride. . . . The tracks went over snow-covered ground with very uneven inclinations in some places. The trail also began and ended on a steep slope coming out and going back into Lake Roosevelt behind the Grand Coulie Dam."

Anthropologist John Napier also found the tracks of Old Cripple Foot to be particularly convincing. Writes Napier, "It is very difficult to conceive of a hoaxer so subtle, so knowledgeable—and so sick—who would deliberately fake a footprint of this nature. I suppose it is possible, but it is so unlikely that I am prepared to discount it."

Meanwhile, Ivan Marx claimed that he was able to actually track the movements of Old Cripple Foot. Its footprints were very easy to recognize, and he found further tracks behind Lake Roosevelt. He followed them and says he actually located several alleged Sasquatch nests, described as groups of small branches snapped off trees and piled with dried leaves and brush.

In July of 1970 more tracks appeared on the beach at North Gorge campground. The tracks showed that Old Cripple Foot had moved in and out of the water, apparently trying to catch the carp which were plentiful in that area.

Marx continued to track the creatures. He claimed to have found bushes that they had eaten from, places where they had slept, and even droppings, which they partially buried. On one occasion he followed the tracks and saw the creature, which he said was 10 feet tall and extremely thin. He believed that it was extremely old. Ivan also claimed to have filmed the creature. When he refused to release the film, he was accused of hoaxing. Despite this, more evidence continued to surface from other areas.

Because of the distinctive nature of the tracks, Old Cripple Foot was easy to identify. As news of the tracks spread, a farmer in northeastern Washington came forward and declared that he had seen the same exact tracks 20 years earlier. In 1976, six years after the flap, Old Cripple Foot turned up again. A college student came upon another line of the unique tracks 40 miles south of the original tracks and immediately contacted investigators. Before long more reports in the same area came in. It seemed that Old Cripple Foot, despite his deformity, was still alive and well.[3]

Today, recorded Bigfoot encounters number in the several thousands, with dozens of new cases coming in each year. The great majority of these encounters are very brief, perhaps involving a simple sighting of a Bigfoot crossing the road at night, peeking into a window, or walking across a field and dashing off into the forest. Most interesting are the extensive cases, involving numerous witnesses with interaction between the Bigfoot and the witnesses, and, of course, lots of evidence.

4

Extensive Encounters

Imagine you are walking along in a field by your home when suddenly you can't believe your eyes. You see an eight-foot-tall figure covered with hair run across your path. You run home to tell everyone, only to find that you're not the only one. Numerous other people are also seeing the creature. Suddenly a single encounter has turned into an extensive encounter involving multiple witnesses. Investigators sometimes call these encounters "waves" because they involve a large number of cases over a short period of time.

Extensive cases produce much more information than the shorter cases, allowing researchers to use them to help understand and solve the mystery of the Bigfoot phenomenon. One such extensive case is that of Old Yellow Top.

OLD YELLOW TOP

In 1909 a group of miners at the Violet Mine in Cobalt, Ontario, Canada, observed a tall, man-like creature. Its entire body was covered with brown hair, except for the top of its head, which had a thick mane of bright yellow hair. All of the witnesses agreed on the appearance of the creature, but nobody knew exactly what it was. The account made its way into the local papers, where reporters quickly nicknamed the mysterious creature "Old Yellow Top."

For a decade and a half, there were no further confirmed sightings. Then, 17 years later, Old Yellow Top made his second major appearance. Again the witnesses were a group of miners working a local mine outside of Cobalt. They observed what they thought was a bear, except it appeared to be picking berries. One of the miners threw a stone at the creature.

Another miner, Mr. Wilson, said, "It kind of stood up and growled at us. Then it ran away. It sure was like no bear that I have ever seen. Its head was kind of yellow, and the rest of it was black like a bear, all covered with hair."

Following this, Old Yellow Top seemed to disappear, until 23 years later, when he returned. On April 16, 1946, a woman and her son were walking along the railroad tracks that led into Cobalt when she saw a hairy, man-like creature with a head of bright blond hair walk "almost like a man" into the forest.

In 1976, yet another 30 years later, Old Yellow Top made one final appearance. A bus driver and 27 miners on their way to work the Cobalt mine observed Old Yellow Top as the creature crossed the road in front of them.

Says the bus driver, Aimee Latreille, "At first I thought it was a big bear. But then it turned to face the headlights and I could see some light hair, almost down to its shoulders. It couldn't have been a bear . . . I have heard of this thing before, but never believed it. Now I am sure."

The 1976 sighting of Old Yellow Top, if true, would mean that the creature was more than 70 years old, unless of course, there is more than one Bigfoot with a yellow mane inhabiting the same area, which doesn't seem very likely. Whatever its age, Old Yellow Top is one of the only cases in which the same individual Sasquatch has been seen multiple times over a period of decades.[1]

THE FOUKE MONSTER

In 1965, 14-year-old Lynn Crabtree went out squirrel hunting near his home in Boggy Creek, Arkansas, as he had done many times before.

As he walked down the forested path he noticed that the local horses and dogs were acting strange. Then, ahead of him on the trail, appeared an eight-foot-tall creature covered with reddish-brown hair. It stood upright like a man, but had extremely long arms. Its face was also covered with hair, showing a long dark, flat nose. The Bigfoot stared at Crabtree for a few moments and then began to walk directly toward him. Crabtree raised his 20-gauge rifle and fired three quick shots. He then turned and raced home as fast as he could. Once safely inside, he quickly told his father, Smokey Crabtree, what he saw.

The father and son returned to the site, but by then the creature was gone. They did, however, find several large, three-toed footprints. They began to wonder if the strange creature could be responsible for the recent unexplained losses of chickens, goats, and pigs in the area. As Lynn Crabtree's story spread, several other local residents also revealed their encounters. There had been at least three recent sightings, and shortly after Lynn Crabtree's encounter, another 14-year-old boy saw the same creature and also shot at it with his shotgun. The Crabtrees and many of their neighbors were farmers and couldn't afford the loss of their livestock. They decided to hunt for the creature.

At the same time, other people began to report encounters. Within a few weeks of Lynn Crabtree's encounter, a Mrs. Ford, who lived in the Fouke area with her husband, Bobby, was sleeping on her sofa in the living room when she was awakened by strange noises. It was a warm evening so the window was open. Looking up, she was shocked to see the curtain moving on the window and a hand come through the opening. Describing her encounter, she said, "At first I thought it was a bear's paw, but it didn't look like that."

At that point the strange intruder showed its face, and she noted its eyes, which looked like "coals of fire–real red."

Mrs. Ford screamed in terror. Mr. Bobby Ford rushed into the room. Both saw the creature turn and run away on two feet. They describe it as "about six feet tall, black and hairy."

That wasn't the end of the encounter. Later that evening Mr. Ford decided to walk around his house and check to see if anything was amiss. Suddenly, the creature lunged up and grabbed him from behind.

The man was so terrified that he managed to free himself from the creature's grip. He ran back into his house so fast that he didn't bother to open the front screen door, but just ran right through it.

Meanwhile, the Crabtree family called together friends and relatives and began the search for the Bigfoot. Although they searched the local area thoroughly, they found no evidence of the creature.

Newspapers heard about the story, and suddenly it became front-page news. Boggy Creek was a very rural area. The nearest town was called Fouke, and before long, hundreds of people were clogging the streets of the small town, inquiring about the "Fouke monster." Following the initial wave of sightings, a motion picture production company arrived on the scene, and soon filming began for a movie about the incident called, *The Legend of Boggy Creek*.

Meanwhile, the sightings continued. In 1966 a local lady who was deer hunting saw the creature. Around the same time a school bus driver saw it cross the road. Residents often heard it screaming in the woods.

In June 1971 the creature left hundreds of footprints in a bean field. The prints were 13½ inches long and 4½ inches wide. Again, the footprints had only three toes. Says Smokey Crabtree, who examined the tracks, "They were so plain you could see the imprint of the lines on the bottom of the bare feet." Crabtree measured the creature's stride at 57 inches. They followed the tracks, but they appeared to wander aimlessly through the field, finally returning into the forest. Crabtree estimated that the creature was probably 300 pounds, judging from the depth of the tracks in the soil.

The movie, *The Legend Of Boggy Creek*, appeared in 1972 and was a semi-fictionalized dramatization of the events that took place. Although it had a very low budget, the film became a cult classic and helped popularize the idea of an unknown, hairy primate living in the backcountry of rural America.

Meanwhile, there was apparently too much activity in Fouke for the Bigfoot. After 1972 there were no further reports. The creature, it appeared, had moved on to a different location.[2]

MOMO, THE MISSOURI MONSTER

At 3:30 p.m., on July 11, 1972, eight-year-old Terry Harrison was playing outside his home in rural Missouri when he saw a large creature walk by the house. He described it as "a big hairy thing with a dog under his arm." Terry screamed for his sister, Doris, age 15. Doris ran outside in time to see the creature standing in the ditch next to their home. Moments later, it ran off into the forest.

Doris ran inside and told her father, Edgar Harrison, what she saw. She described it as "a terrible thing, a monster standing on two legs like a man! It was holding a dog in its arms." The dog appeared to be deceased.

Her father ran outside with his shotgun and took off after the creature. He could hear something crashing through the trees, but he didn't see the creature. He did find some strange, three-toed tracks. The Harrisons also smelled a terrible odor hanging around the house.

The Harrisons called the police and reported their sighting. Edgar Harrison said, "The sheriff checked to see if an ape had maybe escaped from a zoo or traveling circus, but none had. We're just stuck with a mystery I guess. It's spooky being that close to something unknown."

The story of what happened to the Harrisons quickly spread through their local town, and soon several other people came forward claiming to have seen the creature. So began the wave of sightings of a creature known as "Momo, the Missouri Monster." There were actually only a few encounters with the creature over a period of less than a month, but they received a lot of publicity, making Momo one of the most famous Bigfoot cases of the year. Following the mini-wave of sightings, the activity stopped.[3]

THE FLORIDA SKUNK-APE

In February 1971 a group of archaeologists were camping in the Big Cypress Swamp in the Florida Everglades. At around 3 a.m. one of the men, H. C. Osbon, was woken up by the sound of heavy footsteps approaching his tent. He looked outside and saw an incredible sight: an eight-foot-tall, man-like figure stood only a few feet away. His body was covered with light brown hair and he smelled "awful." After a few moments the figure walked away.

The next morning the group found huge footprints measuring 17½ inches long and 11 inches wide. Amazed, they brought in more people to investigate. Over the next few weeks they found more footprints. Later, L. Frank Hudson, who joined the investigation, also saw one of the creatures.

Sasquatch on the Silver Screen

It's late at night and you're driving through the forest with your family. Suddenly a dark figure looms ahead of you on the road. You slam your car brakes, but it's too late. You can't avoid it. With a sickening thud, your car slams into the figure, knocking it down. You jump out of the car and realize that the worst has happened–you have killed it.

Then you wonder something else–what *exactly* have you killed? It's not a person. It's not a bear. It's not a gorilla. What is it? Then you smell it–an awful smell, and you suddenly realize what it is–an actual Sasquatch!

Sound incredible? Tell that to the Henderson family who, after colliding with a Sasquatch, tie it to the roof of their car and take it home. So begins the Hollywood movie, *Harry and the Hendersons*. After taking the creature home, the family learns that the Sasquatch is actually alive. At first the Sasquatch wreaks havoc in their home. However, over time the Hendersons make friends with the creature, and learn to accept and love "Harry," almost as a member of the family. The film was released in 1987 and was an immediate success, eventually earning more than $21 million and starting its own television series.

Harry and the Hendersons is arguably the most famous Bigfoot movie ever made, but it's not the first. One of the earliest fictional treatments

Around this time other people in the vast Florida Everglades also began to report encounters. One of the most dramatic came from an anonymous truck driver, who said that he had pulled over on the side of Interstate Highway 75 to rest. It was a warm evening so he opened the door to let in some air. Suddenly, the truck driver heard footsteps approaching. He turned on the headlights. At that moment a Bigfoot suddenly appeared. It ran up to him, grabbed his legs and pulled him out of the truck. The man fought to free himself of the creature. As he reported, "My blows had no effect. The thing just tucked me under

of Bigfoot was the docudrama *The Legend of Boggy Creek*. Released in 1972 the low-budget film, which was based on actual events in Fouke, Arkansas, became an unexpected and huge success. Filmed on location at Boggy Creek, the film introduced millions of people to Bigfoot, and inspired many professional Bigfoot researchers to begin their own investigations. The film was followed by two sequels, and a number of other Bigfoot movies, most of which flopped at the box office.

Harry and the Hendersons and *The Legend of Boggy Creek* still remain the two most popular Bigfoot movies. However, today Bigfoot has saturated the media and become a part of the culture. Its image is used even in television commercials, advertising everything from car tires to beef jerky. If you still can't get enough Sasquatch, here are some more movies for you:

- *Bigfoot* (1970) (Drama)
- *Little Bigfoot* (1997) (Drama)
- *Sasquatch Oddysey: The Hunt For Bigfoot* (1999) (Documentary)
- *Sasquatch Hunters* (2005) (Horror)
- *Sasquatch Mountain* (2007) (Thriller)
- *The Sasquatch Gang* (2008) (Comedy)

one of his arms like a rag doll . . . My head was pushed down into the fur, and I almost gagged from the stench." The Bigfoot carried him for a few feet and then suddenly released him. The trucker jumped back in his truck and drove away in fear.

These and other encounters found their way into the newspapers, and the Florida Skunk-Ape became a media sensation. Reporters soon learned that the area had a long history of encounters with the creature. It went by many different names, including Squattam's Growlers, the Sandmen, Buggers, and the Abominable Florida Ape-man.

Once the word of the creature was out, large numbers of people began to report their own encounters. In 1974 a man said he struck a Bigfoot with his car while driving through the Everglades near Hollywood, Florida. "I just couldn't avoid hitting it. I hit it on the leg with my front fender. It didn't scream or make any sound." Shortly later, another witness saw what may have been the same Bigfoot in the same area "limping" across the road. Like many witnesses, he insisted upon anonymity.

That same year a security guard at Palm Beach shot six times at an approaching Bigfoot with his gun. As he says, "It was huge–about 7 feet tall–and was real hairy. . . . It smelled like it had taken a bath in rotten eggs."

The encounters continued on a yearly basis and are still going on today. In 1999 a hunter observed one of the creatures walking past him as he hid in a tree. He said the creature was nine feet tall and must have weighed at least 500 pounds.

One of the most exciting recent encounters occurred in the year 2000 near the Myakka River in Sarasota, Florida. An elderly woman, who would not give her name, noticed that someone or something was stealing apples from her back porch at night. One evening she heard a strange "whoomp" noise coming from the backyard. She went outside with her camera to investigate. To her shock, she saw a muscular, reddish-haired, shaggy-looking creature hiding behind her Palmetto plants. She quickly snapped two photographs and ran inside. After the creature left, a strong odor hung in the air.

Figure 4.1 *This drawing of an ape-man resembles the creature described by an elderly woman in Florida in 2000.* (Fortean Picture Library)

The woman sent the photographs with a letter to the local sheriff. Later, Bigfoot researchers learned of the case and the photographs, which have now been extensively examined. No evidence of a hoax has been found. Other than the photographs, however, there is no other evidence proving the existence of the creature. Some investigators have raised the possibility that it was an orangutan that had escaped from a zoo or from a private collector. There were no official reports of any missing orangutans, though, so the mystery remains.

Investigators now believe that the Florida Everglades is a prime habitat for the hairy creatures. Leading cryptozoologist Loren Coleman lists the Florida Everglades as one of the leading locations in the world to have a Bigfoot/Skunk-Ape encounter.[4]

MAKING FRIENDS WITH BIGFOOT

Born in 1912 Datus Perry has lived most of his life in the very rural area above the Columbia River, outside of Carson, Washington. From a young age Perry spent his time roaming the forests and mountains. In 1933 he went on a clam-digging trip on Pacific Beach. One morning he walked up the beach looking for berries and saw that the local bushes had all been picked clean. Looking down he saw a very large, human-like footprint. He knew exactly what the track meant. He had heard other local people talking about their own encounters with tall, hairy ape-men, but he wasn't sure if he believed them. It had to be one of the creatures. Little did he know, he would soon have more encounters.

Perry says his first of many firsthand encounters with Bigfoot occurred in 1937. The creature stood in full view 200 feet ahead of him on a mountain trail. Years later, in 1963, he was hiking along Gifford Peak when he had a second encounter with Bigfoot. On this occasion, it approached within 20 feet and actually followed him down the trail.

From this point Perry started to encounter the creatures on a regular basis. He said that they ranged between 8 and 11 feet tall, had broad shoulders, no visible neck, and a pointed head. He observed them eating fruit, rodents, worms, and other creatures. Perry reported, "They live in mountain alder and in willow, where there's good cover overhead, and where the sun doesn't come out too much. They keep hiding better, going farther away."

Perry said he has encountered the Sasquatch on dozens of occasions, and that they eventually became so used to his presence that they would allow him to approach. "I've been screamed, chattered, whistled, yodeled and knocked at by Sasquatch . . . I have fallen into a lot of experiences with Bigfoot. I think it was meant to be that way, so I could tell you about it."

Perry claimed that he had seen them walking around, hunting and eating, and also just lying around sunning themselves and even sleeping. He said that they used rocks to hunt and could run faster than all the local animals. He believed that the bad odor from some Bigfoot didn't come from the creature, but from the carcasses that they feast upon. During a few of his encounters, he held up offerings such as flowers, tree branches, and fruit, and the Bigfoot approached and took them from his hands.

On one occasion, he had a screaming match with a Bigfoot; it would scream and he would answer. When asked if he had ever heard anything resembling speech, Perry replied, "I've heard them talk five times, but it sure ain't my language: more like Asiatics or something . . . I've been hoping I could make a breakthrough and talk at them . . . but what the heck, I might get friendly with them and then I'd have to tell people about it. They'd think I was really crazy then."

As of 1995 Perry still claimed to be encountering Bigfoot. He is considered to have been an expert by some and a teller of tall tales by others. In either case, his stories have become well known in the field of Bigfoot research. The details of Sasquatch behavior he described are consistent with the accounts reported by other people.

In 1998 a resident of Cumberland County in Tennessee revealed that he had actually formed a relationship with a number of Bigfoot creatures that were apparently living in the Hiwasse Wildlife Refuge.

The gentleman explained that while hiking in the wilderness area over a period of several months, he had a number of encounters with Bigfoot. In one incident he came upon a large group of the creatures. He counted at least 15 of them. They were all covered with dark-brown fur from head to toe and ranged in size between seven and eight feet tall. One was slightly taller and had grayish fur. He appeared to be the leader and would communicate to the other Bigfoot with strange vocal sounds.

The witness said that he began to leave apples in the areas where he had seen the Bigfoot, and after a while, the Bigfoot actually became used to his presence. On one occasion, one of the Bigfoot approached him and took an apple directly from his hand. Unfortunately, the witness had to move from the area and was unable to continue his relationship with the Bigfoot. If true, his case is one of the biggest sightings of multiple Bigfoot on record.[5]

Wild Ape-Men Across the World

In March of 1942, a group of five men hiked through the Himalayan foothills on their way to India. The men had escaped from a *gulag*, a Russian prison-labor camp, and had walked hundreds of miles across the country through treacherous wilderness. They were finally coming out of the mountains and approaching their destination, but they were still in a very remote area. Looking ahead of them on a snowfield, one of the men noticed two figures moving back and forth about a quarter mile away. Having encountered no other living creatures in the mountains, the men were intrigued and hiked forward to investigate. When they approached within a hundred yards of the figures, the men suddenly became silent and looked on in shock. There were two enormous hairy beasts, walking around on two legs like human beings.

One of the men, Slavomir Rawicz, later wrote about what he saw: "Two points struck me immediately. They were enormous and they walked on their hind legs. The picture is clear in my mind . . . we just could not believe what we saw at first, so we stayed to watch . . . I set myself to estimating their height on the basis of my military training for artillery observation. They could not have been much less than eight feet tall. One was a few inches taller than the other."

One of the group suggested they approach closer, but the idea was vetoed when someone else said, "They look strong enough to eat us."

They kept waiting for the creatures to fall down on all fours and walk like a bear, but they never did. Instead, they remained standing on two legs for at least two hours.

During that time the men were able to observe the creatures in detail. Rawicz wrote, "The heads were squarish and ears must lie close to the skull because there was no projection from the silhouette against the snow. The shoulders sloped down to a powerful chest. The arms were long and the wrists reached the level of the knees . . . We decided unanimously that we were examining a type of creature of which we had no previous experience in the wild, in zoos or in literature. . . . There was something of both the bear and the ape about their general shape but they could not be mistaken for either."

For some reason, the Himalayan Mountains appear to contain the highest concentration of these alleged creatures, the Yeti and the Abominable Snowman. Researchers speculate that this is because the environment is largely untouched by industrial development and has remained an inaccessible wilderness for thousands of years. In other words, it is not only the perfect place for a population of primitive ape-men to hide, but to thrive.

In 1957 wealthy businessman Tom Slick (also a well-known Bigfoot hunter) turned his attention to the Yeti and launched an expedition in the Arun Valley in the Himalayas of Nepal. Slick and his party were able to locate alleged hair and dung samples of the creature. A few members of the expedition also claimed to have seen the creature.

In 1959 a young Sherpa called Da Tempa was walking at night along the bank of a stream in the Arun Valley in the Himalayas of Nepal. Da Tempa saw a figure about four and a half feet tall wading in the stream. He shined his flashlight on the creature and was shocked to see that it was a Yeti. The creature quickly ran away on two legs. The next morning the creature's tracks were found at the site.

In 1972 biologists Edward Cronin and Jeffrey McNeely were conducting surveys in the same Arun Valley of Nepal. They made their camp high on a ridge, directly below a mountain pass that led to the next valley. When they woke up the team discovered fresh nine-inch tracks of an ape-like creature that walked on two legs. The tracks showed that sometime during the night the creature had been walking along the ridgeline, then veered into their campsite and walked around the various tents. A few members of the team followed the tracks backward and discovered that they came from a steep slope, which the creature had ascended with apparent ease. Other members followed the tracks forward and observed that the creature, after walking among the tents, returned back to the ridgeline and into the next valley. The men couldn't follow the tracks any farther, as they became lost among the boulders, but they did take photographs of the tracks. When they returned their story and photographs caused a media sensation and helped to renew interest in the Yeti.

In 1979 mountaineers John Edwards and John Allen were not even looking for the Yeti when they apparently came upon its lair. They were at 17,000-feet elevation in the Himalayas when they spotted what looked like an ideal campsite with an "overhanging boulder that formed a natural cave." As Allen approached he noticed a set of nearly human-looking footprints in the snow. At that moment both men were startled by "a piercing, chilling, inhuman scream that lasted five or ten seconds."

Edwards and Allen left the area, but returned the next day with their entire team to investigate and take photographs of the footprints. The leader of the team, John Whyte, said, "We have photographed a print that no one can satisfactorily explain. I am convinced that there is an animal up there that is not yet recorded by naturalists." Team members also found strange droppings near the prints that were gathered and taken back to England for analysis.

Although numerous reports of Yeti have come from the Himalayas, the creature and those similar to it are in no way confined to just Tibet and Nepal. In fact, reports of strange primates come from across the world, including South America, Africa, Europe, England, Asia, and Australia. While the types of ape-men seem to vary, the reports are basically the same, involving mysterious and powerful human-like beasts.[1]

RUSSIAN APE-MEN

In 1925 thousands of Russian troops marched into the Vanch Mountains of the Pamir region. As they traveled through the countryside, the locals warned them to be wary of "beast-men," who lived in the higher elevations.

According to researcher Odette Tchernine, the Soviet soldiers were amazed to find numerous tracks and other evidence of the feared beast-men. One day a group of soldiers came upon a large cave. Thinking that the enemy might be hiding inside, they fired blindly into the cave. Suddenly a "wild, hairy creature" ran out. It was instantly killed by a barrage of machine gunfire. The leader of the troop, General Mikhail Stepanovich Topilskiy examined the creature and could clearly see that it was not an ape. Instead it looked almost human. General Topilskiy said, "It was covered with fur. But I knew there were no apes in the Pamirs, and moreover, the body looked far more human than ape-like, indeed fully human."

The medical officer conducted a closer examination and concluded that the creature was neither human nor ape, but apparently a mixture of both. The corpse was that of a male creature, about 5½ feet tall, covered with dense, gray-brown hair except for the face, ears, palms, knees, feet, and buttocks. The skin in these areas was dark, rough, and callused. The teeth were abnormally large but looked human. The chest was also unusually muscular but very human-like.

Unable to preserve or carry the corpse, the soldiers gave it a human burial, covering it with a large pile of stones.

In 1941 an apparent wild-man was captured by locals in the mountains near Buinaksk. Soviet Army Lieutenant Colonel V. S. Karapetyan was asked to examine the wild-man to determine if he might be a spy. Karapetyan was also a medical officer, and officials requested his expertise in identifying the alleged wild-man.

The colonel was shocked at what he saw. As he said, "I can still see the creature as it stood before me, a male, naked and barefoot. It was doubtless a man, because its entire shape was human. The chest, back and shoulder, however were covered with shaggy hair of a dark brown color... The man stood absolutely straight with his arms hanging, and his height was above average (about six feet.) He stood before me like a giant, his mighty chest thrust forward. His fingers were thick, strong and exceptionally large. On the whole, he was considerably bigger than any of the local inhabitants. He eyes told me nothing. They were dull and empty—the eyes of an animal."

The colonel examined the man-creature further and finally concluded that, whoever the man was, he was neither a spy nor a normal human being. Said Karapetyan, "This was no disguised person, but a wild-man of some kind."

In 1957 A. G. Pronin (a hydrologist from Leningrad University) looked around him to select a campsite. He was in the middle of the very isolated Pamir Mountains in the Soviet Union on a technical mission. Looking across the ravine, he was shocked to see a "man-like" figure standing on a cliff top. The figure had hunched shoulders, long arms, and was covered with reddish-gray hair. After a few moments it walked away with big strides. A few days later Pronin sighted the creature again. He was convinced that the creature, whatever it was, was not human. He later learned that the local villagers and Kirhgiz herdsmen were very familiar with the creature. They called it "Guli-avan" or "Golub-yavan" which translates literally into "wild-man."

Numerous other accounts come from the Soviet Union. In the 1960s researcher Marie-Jeanne Koffman and her team collected more than 500 eyewitness accounts of wild-man sightings, the majority of which originated from the Caucasus Mountains. The natives there call the creature Almas or Almasty. Koffman heard reports from peasants, villagers, tea-pickers, haymakers, and other local inhabitants who all gave the same description. They said the creatures looked almost human and were of average human height. They had a receding brow and chin and a flat nose. They were usually covered with thick red hair, and had very muscular bodies, with no apparent neck, and long muscular arms.

Figure 5.1 *An artist's rendering of a wild-man trudging down the slope of a snowy mountain.* (Fortean Picture Library)

One of Koffman's most exciting discoveries was finding two apparent wild-man nests, which were hidden in thickets of brush. In the nests they found a pile of food that the creature had collected. The larder included two pumpkins, a pile of blackberries, eight potatoes, a sunflower, the remains of three already eaten apples, and a half-chewed corncob. Interestingly, they also found pellets of horse dung, which the Almas allegedly enjoyed because of its high salt content. Although no wild-man was found, investigators studied teeth marks on the corncob, which showed that the jaw was much wider than that of a human being.[2]

CHINESE WILD-MEN

In 1954 Chinese film director Pai Hsin of the Chinese People's Army was returning from a trip to the Himalayas. He and his crew hiked through the Pamir Mountains of northern China at an elevation of about 19,600 feet. It was very early morning when Hsin and several others observed two man-like figures walking "one behind the other up a slope." The figures were short and hunched over but walked with ease across the rough landscape. Hsin and the others shouted and fired gunshots into the air to attract attention, but the two figures ignored them and walked quickly away. After hearing that the area was well known for "wild-men," Pai Hsin realized that they had encountered two of them.

One afternoon in May of 1957, a small village in the east China province of Zhejiang experienced a dramatic attack by an unknown ape-man. All the men were working in the nearby hills, and the women were alone in the village. Xu Fidi was in her home when she suddenly heard her young daughter screaming in terror. She ran outside where her daughter was tending cattle and was shocked to see her struggling in the grip of a hairy ape-man nearly five feet tall, covered with long, dark-brown hair, and with a human-like face. Xu Fidi grabbed a stick and began to strike the creature. After a few moments, the creature released its grip and sprang off into a nearby rice paddy field.

By this time Xu Fidi's daughter's screams had attracted all the women in town, who upon seeing what was happening, picked up sticks and attacked the ape-man. Together with Xu Fidi, they beat it to death with their sticks.

They then cut up the creature, saving only its hands and feet which were carefully preserved by Zhou Shousong, a young biology teacher from a nearby village. Meanwhile, news of the strange event spread like wildfire. Soon reporters came to the village, asking for more information. According to reporters from the *Sonyang Daily*, the creature was a young male weighing 88 pounds. It had a large chest, a sunken nose, and large white teeth. It was covered from head to toe with long brown hair. Underneath the hair, its skin was soft and white. In every other way, it appeared human.

Later, Chinese investigators obtained the preserved hands and feet of the creature from Zhou Shousong. The feet were covered with soft, yellow-brown hair and measured 7½ inches long. The palms of the hands were hairless and measured 5½ inches long. The conclusion was that the hands and feet belonged to some kind of unknown primate. It seemed most closely related to chimpanzee.

To Zhang Qilin of Xikiangli Village, the Yeti is not a myth but a daily reality. It is his job to guard the local maize crop against the ape-men, who often come down out of the mountains to feed on the corn. He has guarded the crop for more than 30 years and has had several face-to-face encounters. In 1970 he had a very close encounter when he saw one in the fields. Said Qilin, "It was about as high as a house door and it was covered in reddish-brown hair with long hair falling around its shoulders and over its face. It walked upright."

Later he had another encounter when he saw an ape-man lying in a tree, eating corn that it had just robbed from his field. Qilin reported, "It was quite relaxed and it clapped its hands when it saw me. Most of the time it just lay there, eating maize. There was a big pile of cobs on the ground."

In the mid-1970s a wave of wild-man sightings occurred in the Hubei Province in China. One famous encounter occurred in May 1976.

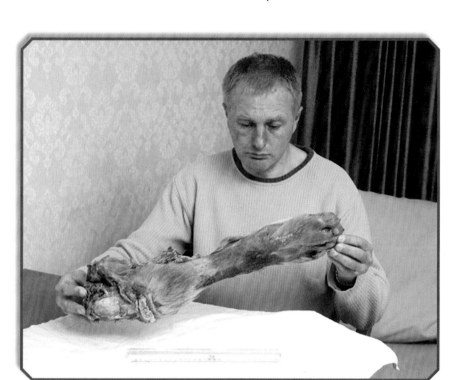

Figure 5.2 *Russian scientist Serghiei Semionov displays the leg of an unknown animal, perhaps a Yeti, in this January 2004 photograph.* (epa/Corbis)

As six communist party members were driving through the province their driver suddenly saw a large, hairy figure crouched on the road ahead. The driver honked his horn and the creature tried to run away, but was unable to scale the cliff next to the road. Everyone in the car jumped out and started to surround the creature. They all got a good look at it and described it as having soft, fine hair like a camel's, with a dark red streak running down its back. It had long, muscular legs and soft-soled feet. It had a long, broad face, with a wide mouth a narrow chin. Realizing it was becoming trapped, the creature stood up on two legs and dashed away in long, loping strides.

One month later, on June 19, 1976, also in the Hubei Province, Gong Gulan had run out of grass to feed her pigs, so she took her four-year-old son and climbed up the mountain near her home to

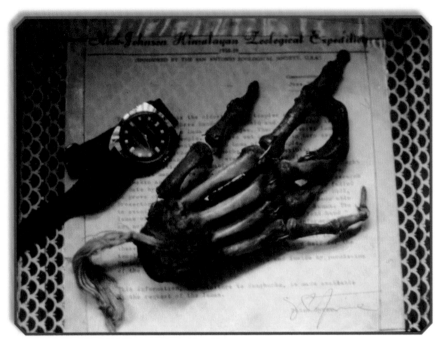

Figure 5.3 *The remains of an alleged Yeti hand.* (Fortean Picture Library)

gather a supply. Looking about 20 feet ahead of her on the path, she was shocked to see a red-haired, human-looking ape-creature scratching its back against a tree trunk. Said Gong Gulan, "It stood, just like a man." Realizing what she was seeing, she scooped up her son, turned around and ran back home. To her horror, the creature began to chase her, emitting loud cries that sounded like, "Ya-ya!"

Gong ran a quarter mile home and ran inside for safety. Her husband said, "When Gong arrived, the beads of sweat on her forehead were as big as soybeans. She kept saying, 'wild-man!'"

Scientists later interviewed Gong about her case and were even able to gather hair samples from the tree trunk where the creature had scratched itself. Scientists at the Beijing Medical Institute examined the hairs and concluded that they were not from a bear but appeared to be similar to those "of the higher primates, including man."

By this time reports of wild-man had become so common in the provinces of Hubei, Shaanxi, and Sichuan that the Chinese Academy of Sciences in Peking decided to organize an official search. In March of 1977 the academy sent a 110-member expedition composed of biologists, zoologists, photographers, soldiers, hunting dogs, and the latest technological recording equipment. Zhou Guoxing, of the Peking Museum of Natural History, was put in charge of the expedition, which lasted for eight months.

The results of the expedition were astonishing. Although they didn't capture the creature itself, they did find considerable evidence. As reported in the *New York Times* on January 5, 1980:

> Many footprints, 12 to 16 inches long were found. Feces, sometimes found beside the footprints and presumed to be from the creature, was analyzed and found to be from neither a human nor a bear, according to Mr. Zhou. Hair samples, believed to have come from the animal and found stuck to tree bark, suggest that it is some sort of higher primate, he said. From accumulated evidence, including purported witnesses, Mr. Zhou describes the creature as about six feet six inches tall, covered with wavy red hair, with the hair on its head falling nearly to its waist . . . The creature is believed to be **omnivorous**, but is said to prefer walnuts and chestnuts, tender young leaves and roots, and insects. While no recording exists of its calls, those who have heard it say it emits one long and one short cry.

After studying all the reports of the wild-man, Zhou Guoxing speculated that the wild-men might be descendents of a supposedly extinct primate known as Meganthropus, which he describes as a "giant ape-man that died out because it lacked sufficient intelligence to adapt to its environment."

In late 1980 another team of Chinese scientists explored the Zhe-jiang province for evidence of living ape-men. As a guide they hired a local herb-picker, who knew the area very well. With the help of their guide, the team located what it believes to be no less than 11 separate Yeti nests, most of which were in an area called Fengshuyang. Some were in trees and some were on the ground, but each was built with a complicated structure using very heavy logs that only a large and intelligent creature could build. The nests all appeared to be no less than two years old as they were still in good condition. Also, there were footprints and droppings around the structures.

Later, more nests were discovered in the remote area of Nine Dragon Mountains. Footprints around the nests measured 13 inches long.

Whatever the case, the number of reported cases is growing. In 1999 anthropologist Dr. Grover Krantz wrote, "The total number of wild-man reports from China that are currently 'on record,' whatever that means, is now three hundred."[3]

MEXICAN WILD-MEN

In the wilderness areas outside of Chiapas, Mexico, along the border of Guatemala, a type of wild-man has become very well known among the native population. The natives call the creatures different names, including Salvaje, Cax-vinic, or fantasma humano (wild-man or spirit man). The area where this creature was usually seen was so isolated that there were no roads, and it was a three-day journey by riverboat.

In the early 1960s researcher and zoologist Ivan T. Sanderson corresponded with a firsthand witness, an American woman who lived among the natives. After hearing about Sanderson's research into wild ape-men, she wrote him a letter describing her own encounters, and said, "I have seen this creature on various occasions and heard it frequently. The last time was about a year ago . . . I don't think I have ever heard anything so disturbing–not frightening but more dreadful and haunting, and full of threat I couldn't imagine."

Geologist Wendell Skousen was part of a team of scientists who often traveled to this area for botanical and zoological studies. His team had heard strange calls in the night jungle, and wondered if it might be the strange wild-men rumored to inhabit the area. At first the local natives refused to talk, but Skousen persisted. After much questioning, the natives told him that the creatures are, in fact, very real and dangerous. Skousen wrote, "They live in the mountain forest, very big, wild-men, completely clothed in short, thick, brown, hairy fur, with no necks, small eyes, long arms and huge hands. They leave footprints twice the length of a man's."

The natives told Skousen that the creatures usually walked on two legs and were much taller than a man, but they could also travel on all fours. They lived in the higher elevations. The natives were terrified of the creatures and a few claimed to have been chased down the mountains by one. The natives often hear their loud calls in the night. Skousen tried to get some of the local natives to guide him to the areas where the creatures were seen. Only a few of the bravest agreed. Unfortunately, they never encountered the creature.[4]

THE DWENDIS OF CENTRAL AMERICA

With its vast jungles, huge mountains and rain forests, it should come as no surprise that Central America also has a long tradition of strange ape-men inhabiting the wild regions. The country of Honduras, located on the northern tip of Central America, contains many wild and remote areas that produce a steady stream of ape-man reports.

Many of the natives call the creatures Dwendis, after the Spanish word, *duende*, which means "goblin." Researcher Ivan T. Sanderson wrote, "I talked to innumerable people there about them. Dozens told me of having seen them, and they were mostly men of substance who worked for responsible organizations like the Forestry Department . . . One, a junior forestry officer born locally, described in great detail two of these little creatures that he had suddenly noticed quietly watching him on several occasions at the edge of the forestry reserve near the foot of the Maya Mountains."

All the witnesses to the Dwendis describe the same type of creature. Sanderson said, "These little folk were described as being between three foot six and four foot six, well proportioned but with very heavy shoulders and rather long arms; clothed in thick, tight, close, brown hair looking like that of a short-coated dog; having very flat yellowish faces but head hair no longer than the body hair, except down the back of the neck."

The Dwendis have been seen not only in Honduras, but also in Belize, the West Indies, and Nicaragua. They do not use tools or speak, but they have often been seen holding large broad leaves as if for camouflage or to protect them from the sun. They are very shy, but also curious, and many witnesses have also reported seeing them stealing and carrying dogs.[5]

SOUTH AMERICAN WILD-MEN

Throughout the 1950s and 1960s German zoologist and exotic animal dealer Claus U. Oheim explored the wild jungles in the South American countries of Ecuador and Colombia, where he obtained many of his specimens. This area is the location of the Pacific slope of the huge Andes mountain range. At the time much of this area remained unexplored, so Oheim wasn't too surprised when he began hearing reports of a strange human-ape-like creature that the natives called Shiru.

Oheim wrote, "The so-called Shiru, I have heard of from the Indians and a few white hunters on both sides of the Andes. . . . All reports describe the Shiru as a small, (four to five feet) creature, decidedly **hominid**, but fully covered with short, dark brown fur. All agreed that the Shiru was very shy. . . . These reports were sober and objective and in no way tinged with the color of imagination."

Oheim did hear of one incident in which a hunter was nearly attacked by one of the Shiru. The hunter had come upon one of the creatures and fired at it with his gun. He apparently missed the creature as it turned and charged directly at him, chasing him out of the area.

In 1930 a hunter named Inocencio was part of an expedition of 10 men hunting in the wild jungles of Patagonia in southern Argentina. During the expedition Inocencio became separated from his group and lost in the jungle. When dark arrived and he was still lost, he realized that he would have to find a safe place to spend the night. He found a large tree and climbed up to a fork in the branches and tried to rest. In the middle of the night he was startled by a loud cry of some type of creature. He also heard footsteps coming closer and closer. As the creature approached, it continued to make loud cries Inocencio described as "horrible, deafening and inhuman."

Inocencio peered through the darkness in the direction of the sound. As he said, "Immediately afterwards, there was a loud noise of footsteps, as if a large animal was coming towards me at top speed . . . Finally a silhouette the size of a man of middle height appeared in the clearing."

The hunter said the figure "stood upright like a man" and roared. Inocencio quickly readied his gun and fired, and said, "There was a savage roar and then a noise of crashing bushes. I was alarmed to see the animal growling towards me."

The hunter fired a second shot. The creature retreated a few steps but continued to roar. Inocencio shot at the creature again, and it roared in pain and finally retreated into the forest. In the morning, he found bloodstains. Also, the entire area was covered with a "sour penetrating smell." Inocencio then found his way out and returned to his companions.

The countries of Guyana, Brazil, Venezuela, and others in South America also have a long tradition of wild-men, usually referred to as Didi, or Deedee.

A very early report comes from explorer Sir Walter Raleigh, who heard accounts of strange wild-men inhabiting the jungles, which were written about by Raleigh's chroniclers. In 1769 influential botanist and naturalist Edward Bancroft spoke with the local natives and learned from them of the existence of species of ape-men which lived in the forest, were about five feet tall, walked erect, and were completely covered in black hair.

In 1868 Charles Barrington Brown (a surveyor for the British Government) was assigned to British Guiana. While staying there, he heard "the plaintive moan or howl" of a strange creature coming from the jungles. He asked the local natives about the noises. They explained that the noises were made by a race of hairy ape-men, who lived deep in the forest. The natives described them as short, very strange, and totally covered with hair.

Brown describes the sound of one of the creatures: "We heard a long, and most melancholy whistle, proceeding from the direction of

Theories

If Bigfoot is real, then this raises the question, what type of species is it? All the evidence points toward it being some type of primate. They are clearly not humans. Nor do they appear to match any known species of ape. Skeptics often claim that people are simply misperceiving bears. However, the eyewitness reports and footprint evidence shows that they are not bears because bears are not bipedal, and bear footprints rarely exceed 12 inches. Some researchers speculate that Bigfoot could represent the so-called missing link, which would provide the answers to how humans allegedly evolved from lower primates. Others believe that they could be a species that was previously thought to be extinct. The two most popular theories are that Bigfoot, the Yeti, and other ape-men are either Gigantopithecus (a previously extinct giant primate) or **Neanderthals** (an early type of Homo sapiens).

Gigantopithecus

About 300,000 years ago, a giant 12-foot tall bipedal ape walked the earth along with Homo Erectus, the ancestors of humans. While humans the forest, at which some of the men exclaimed in an awed tone of voice, 'The Didi.' Two or three times the whistle was repeated, sounding like that made by a human being, beginning in a high key and dying slowly and gradually away in a low one."

Brown later interviewed several other people who had firsthand encounters with the Didi, including a magistrate by the name of Mr. Haines who had an encounter in the same area in 1910, while prospecting for gold. Brown wrote, "He suddenly came upon two strange creatures, which stood up on their hind-feet when they saw him. They had human features but were entirely covered with reddish-brown fur . . . The two creatures retreated slowly and disappeared into the forest without once taking their eyes off him."

thrived, the Gigantopithecus reportedly became extinct. The fossil evidence for the existence of Gigantopithecus consists of three jawbones and about a thousand teeth. From these fossils, anthropologists have been able to determine that Gigantopithecus was the largest known primate and that it walked upright on two legs. A large number of leading Sasquatch researchers, including Grover Krantz, Bernard Heuvelmans, Ivan Sanderson, and John Green, have pointed to this species as the most likely explanation for the reports.

Neanderthals

Neanderthals were bipedal primates with human-sized brains, who are known to have used tools and fire. They have been extinct for nearly 100,000 years. Most researchers feel that the Neanderthal does not match Sasquatch reports, particularly because Neanderthals were of average human stature and were not covered all over their body with hair. On the other hand, some researchers have pointed out that some of the ape-man and wild-man reports from China, Russia, and other Eastern countries do seem to match the description of Neanderthals. For this reason, the theory remains popular.

Argentina has also produced reports. In 1956 geologist Audio Pich found several 17-inch-long tracks at an elevation of 16,000 feet. Meanwhile, in 1958, the country of Chile produced a number of reports of enormous, hair-covered creatures roaming through the mountains.[6]

WILD-MEN FROM AFRICA

In 1927 Cuthbert Burgoyne and his wife were on vacation in traveling up the coast of East Africa. Looking at the beach, they saw a large group of baboons sunning themselves. Suddenly they saw "two little brown men" walk out of the bush and among the baboons. Said Burgoyne, "These small human-like animals were probably between four and five feet tall, quite upright and graceful in figure. At the time I was quite thrilled as they were quite evidently no beast of which I had heard or read."

In 1937 Captain William Hichens revealed how, a few years earlier, he was on a lion hunt in East Africa when he had a strange encounter with unknown primates. As he later wrote, "I saw two small, brown furry creatures come from dense forest on one side of the glade and disappear into the thickets on the other. They were like little men, about four feet high, walking upright, but clad in russet hair. The native hunter with me gazed in mingled fear and excitement. They were, he said, *agogwe*, the little furry men whom one does not see once in a lifetime."

In 1947 Professor LeDoux, head of the zoological department of the Institute of Education and Research in Adibjan, Nigeria, in the continent of Africa was shocked to hear that a local native boy had recently spotted a wild man. LeDoux interviewed the witness and learned that he had seen a "little man with long reddish fur and long hair on his head." LeDoux showed the boy photographs of pygmies, but the boy replied that what he saw looked nothing like them. The professor soon learned that the existence of the red-haired dwarfs was well known among the local population. It was considered very bad luck to encounter one. He learned that a large group of workmen had seen one of the wild-men climbing a tall tree one year earlier.

In 1960 Nyasaland game rangers in the forest region of Nkata Bay were overwhelmed by reports of a "black, shaggy monster." Upon investigating, they found more than 30 mysterious treetop structures that they believed to be nests. The local natives called the creature Ufiti. They told the rangers it was five feet tall, broad chested, and covered with long black hair.[7]

AUSTRALIAN YOWIES

One evening in 1912 surveyor Charles Harper was camping with several companions on Currockbilly Mountain in New South Wales, Australia. As they sat around their campfire preparing for bed, strange sounds from a large creature came from the forest around them. Frightened by the loud noises, the men quickly stacked more wood on the fire until it was blazing brightly. That's when they got their first good view of the creature.

As Harper told reporters:

> A huge man-like animal stood erect not twenty yards from the fire, growling and thumping his breast with his huge hand-like paws. I looked round and saw that one of my companions had fainted. . . . The creature stood in one position for some time . . . I should say its height when standing erect would be 5 feet 8 inches to 5 feet 10 inches. Its body, legs and arms were covered with long, brownish-red hair, which shook with every quivering movement of its body . . . What struck me was the apparently human shape, but still so different . . . The body frame was enormous, indicating immense strength and power of endurance. The arms and forepaws were extremely long and large, and very muscular, being covered with shorter hair. The head and face were very small, but very human. The eyes were large, dark and piercing, deeply set.

Harper also noticed two large, protruding canine teeth. The creature growled and thumped its chest a few more times, then walked off for a few yards on two feet, then fell to all fours and ran away. Harper and the others decided to end their camping trip and return to civilization. During the incident, they wondered if they had seen some kind of Australian gorilla. There are no gorillas native to Australia, but the local natives have a long oral history of similar creatures that they call the Yowie.[8]

With so many different types of wild-men and ape-men coming from such a wide variety of locations, many researchers feel that there are likely multiple different species. While it might be convenient to label them all Bigfoot, Yeti, or ape-men, investigators realize that they may be dealing with *dozens* of different species. They all seem to fall under the zoological family known as primates. Otherwise, they vary widely in appearance and are called literally hundreds of different names by the local populations. The only other thing they have in common is that they continue to remain an unsolved mystery.

6

Sasquatch Science

From 1975 to 1977 a wave of Sasquatch sightings hit the area outside of Helena, Montana. Dozens of separate sightings occurred involving scores of witnesses. Several of the incidents were investigated by the local sheriff's office. Officers found footprints measuring 17½ inches long and 7 inches wide and made plaster casts. Another case involved a man who claimed to have shot at one of the creatures with his gun.

As the number of reports grew and the evidence mounted, the story attracted widespread interest and caused controversy. To prove their accounts, several witnesses insisted on being given lie detector tests, which they passed. One reporter wrote in *The Great Falls Tribune*, "So far, none of the monsters had made any move to harm a human. . . . We urge people not to shoot at them with guns, but with cameras. If possible, we'd like to take one alive to study it."

This is only one of many cases involving multiple eyewitnesses and physical evidence. Unknown to many people, there is, in fact, considerable physical evidence to support the existence of Bigfoot, including footprints, hair samples, movie films, and more. Although few in number, several scientists today are taking Sasquatch reports seriously, especially when there is physical evidence available for scientific study. Leading primatologist Jane Goodall is one of many prominent scientists who find the evidence for Bigfoot very convincing. Said Goodall, "Well now you'll be amazed when I tell you that I am sure they exist."[1]

BIGFOOT FOOT PRINTS

Today, most experts believe that footprints provide the best available evidence. Grover Krantz wrote, "The most tangible evidence of the Sasquatch that is currently available consists of footprints." Krantz estimates that there have been more than 100,000 prints reported.[2]

The scientific study of footprints is known as *ichnology*. By studying the tracks of animals, ichnologists are able to learn a lot about all the animals in any particular area, including such important facts as diet, behavior, lifestyle, size and weight of the animal, and more. This unique science has revealed many of the secrets behind Bigfoot.

Size of Footprints

By far the most unusual aspect of Bigfoot prints is their sheer size. Bigfoot prints have been measured longer than 20 inches. The size alone indicates that humans didn't make them, as human footprint size rarely exceeds 12 inches. The only other possibility would be bear, but bear footprints measure only 12 to 14 inches. Gorilla can be ruled out because their footprints are even smaller, and gorilla are not native to the United States, where many Bigfoot prints have been found.

Step Length

Step length is the distance measured from the back edge of one heel print to the mark made by the next footprint, also known as stride length. For humans, this usually measures about two to three feet. However, with Bigfoot, step length averages about four to five feet. This simple fact makes it very easy for the experienced researcher to determine if Bigfoot footprints have been faked, as it is nearly impossible for a human to have such a long stride. Several researchers have pointed out that step length alone can be used to conclusively

Figure 6.1 *Skeptics attribute many Bigfoot reports and tracks to bears. Researchers do not agree, as bear tracks are smaller than Bigfoot tracks and bears cannot walk on two legs for long distances.* (Gail Shumway/Getty Images)

rule out human hoaxing. Interestingly, no hoaxer has ever stepped forward and publicly produced a set of convincing footprints just to show that it could even be done. Until that time, researchers maintain that footprints remain some of the best evidence proving the existence of Bigfoot.

Track Depth

Another key measurement investigators use to determine whether or not a Bigfoot print is real is the depth of the track. The depth of any footprints can be used as a measurement device to approximate the weight of whoever made the footprints. Bigfoot are reportedly very heavy, and therefore genuine tracks should be deeper than normal human tracks. This pattern has turned up in several cases. By trying to duplicate the tracks in the same area, researchers are able to determine the approximate weight of the creature that made the footprints.

Also, footprints from live creatures do not have a uniform depth. Without exception, the toe or the heel digs deeper than the center arch of the foot. In the case of hoaxed Bigfoot prints, however, the tracks are often completely flat, with none of the natural curves that occur in the feet of known primates. When researchers find tracks that contain the variations in depth from heel to toe, they can be reasonably certain that the footprints were made by some type of living creature and were not hoaxed.

One example comes from researcher Grover Krantz. In 1975 he was shown a set of footprints found in southwestern Washington State. After examining the tracks, and then trying to duplicate them, Krantz was able to determine that the tracks were genuine. As he wrote, "My conclusion was that something there had placed those footprints with upwards of 800 pounds of weight coming down on them with no more impact than from a striding gait."[3]

Dermatoglyphics

Probably the most convincing evidence coming from the scientific study of footprints is known as **dermatoglyphics**, or dermal ridges.

Figure 6.2 *A researcher measures the stride length of a set of alleged Bigfoot tracks. The stride length of Bigfoot is reported to be twice that of humans.*
(Fortean Picture Library)

Humans and other primates all have ridges on the skin of their hands and feet. These tiny ridges are unique to the individual. Law enforcement uses fingerprints to identify individuals. In the same way, Sasquatch researchers are now able to determine if Sasquatch prints are real or fake. In some of the better-preserved tracks, researchers have even been able to identify the impressions of individual tiny sweat glands. In other cases, footprints have been distinctive enough to enable researchers to actually track an individual Bigfoot, such as Old Cripple Foot, across a wide area. Again, with hoaxed footprints, there is usually a complete lack of dermal ridges, as this kind of detail is very hard to fake.

BIGFOOT HANDPRINTS

In a few very rare cases, researchers have been able to investigate reports of Bigfoot handprints. In 1972 researcher Ivan Marx researched a site where it appeared that a Bigfoot had sat down on the ground and placed one hand in the mud while using the other to dig. Marx made plaster casts of the handprint, which measured 11.8 inches long and 6.9 inches wide, or nearly twice the size of a human hand. Interestingly, the print showed that the thumb was not opposable, a feature unique to humans that allows them to grasp and manipulate objects more easily. Also, the fingers were much thicker and more widely spaced than human fingers.

Grover Krantz made latex copies of the casts and discovered that they showed dermal ridges, which are again unique to living creatures. Wrote Krantz, "The parallel ridges were oriented just like fingerprints along the edge of the last segment of the second digit, on its thumbward side . . . This is the first-noticed example of dermal ridges being recorded in a Sasquatch print of any kind."

In 1986 Paul Freeman found an incredible set of tracks that showed that a Sasquatch had crossed a stream and fell down as it climbed onto the bank, leaving at least one clear handprint. Freeman made a plaster cast. The hand measured 13 inches long and 9 inches wide. As in other cases, the fingers were again very thick and widely spaced. There were also several 17-inch footprints in the area. Anthropologist Jeff Meldrum examined the casts made of the hand-prints and concluded that they were genuine, in part because they showed lines along the palms known as *flexion creases.* He was also able to determine that the print was not human. Meldrum wrote, "The hand exhibits the more apelike characteristics of relatively flat palm and nonopposable thumb."

In the mid-1980s researcher Bob Titmus was in the forests of northern California searching for evidence of Bigfoot when he made an incredible find. He found a line of clear tracks that led through a gravel bed to a water hole. The evidence showed that the Sasquatch had climbed down into the water hole and then climbed up the muddy bank on its hands and knees. Most of the prints were smeared, except there was one very clear handprint. Titmus photographed the print and showed it to researcher Jeff Meldrum, who wrote, "The most striking feature is the orientation of the thumb imprint. The broad pad of the thumb lies close to the remaining fingers, and its pad is facing in the same direction, rather than rotated toward the palm. Once again, this distinctive anatomy of the nonopposed thumb is evident."[4]

BODY PRINTS

In 1993 Bigfoot researcher Paul Freeman discovered large tracks that led to a sandy area along Dry Creek in Walla Walla, Washington. The area was a well-known hotbed of Bigfoot activity, but Freeman was still surprised at what he found next. The tracks led to the edge of a sandy bank where the Sasquatch apparently sat down in the sand, leaving a distinct imprint of its buttocks. Freeman first measured the butt-print at 14½ inches across. He made a plaster cast that he turned over to investigators. Anthropologist and anatomist Jeff Meldrum studied the cast in detail and is convinced that it's not human. Wrote Meldrum, "The coccyx or tailbone was evident at the commencement of the deep natal cleft. The cheeks of the buttocks were prominent and apparently well muscled. The depth of the imprint and the clarity and width of the natal cleft indicated a well-developed musculature . . . The striations

Please Don't Feed the Bigfoot!

If Bigfoot is real then the question remains, how can such a large creature nourish itself? What exactly does it eat? Luckily, there are many reports of people who have caught Bigfoot in the act of eating. By all reports, it seems to be omnivorous. In other words, it will eat just about anything that's edible.

Grace Hamby has interviewed dozens of people who have encountered Bigfoot across the northwestern United States. According to Hamby, "The creatures like cattail roots, leaves and fruit of huckleberry and wild raspberry, and the inner bark of cottonwood. They also feed on insects, gophers, marmots, rabbits, frogs and fish."

Anthropologist and pioneering Bigfoot researcher John Napier said that in many ways, the Sasquatch has the same diet as a bear. "Observers have seen and reported the Sasquatch eating berries, fruit, leaves, spruce tips, water-plants, tubers, fish, rodents, deer, as well as sheep, cows [and] horses."

Leading researcher Grover Krantz wrote, "In general I would describe the Sasquatch as omnivorous. It is probably mainly a vegetarian and what might be called an 'opportunistic carnivore.' Meat may be its preferred dietary item, but it has no obvious specializations toward any particular game, so it grabs what it can, whenever and however it can.... Any species is fair game."

Jeff Meldrum agrees: "Based on the numerous accounts that mention feeding or carrying food, the Sasquatch diet seems to span the wide spectrum of a generalized omnivore. Eyewitnesses have reported everything from roots and berries to deer and elk...Numerous credible eyewitnesses recount seeing Sasquatch dispatch and carry off adult deer as well as fawns."

of hair could be seen streaming downward and inward . . . this cast was quite anatomically correct and yet distinctly nonhuman in dimension and proportion."

Bigfoot expert Dr. Bindernagel wrote, "Many Sasquatch sightings come from clam beaches. West Coast clam beaches are incredibly rich in terms of shellfish, marine worms and other forms of animal protein. I think one day we will come to accept that the West Coast beaches are one of the best Sasquatch habitats in North America."

The many cases of rock-throwing Bigfoot would seem to indicate that Bigfoot are also efficient hunters, and in fact, several cases exist in which people have seen Bigfoot throwing rocks at animals. Also, there are many cases on record in which Bigfoot has raided chicken coops, stripped fruit trees, or even stolen food from campers and picnickers.

In a few other cases people have actually fed a Bigfoot. In 1966 a couple living in a rural area of Burlington County, New Jersey, woke up one morning and found several 17-inch-long footprints outside their home. A few days later they observed the hairy face of a Sasquatch staring at them through a window that was more than seven feet above the ground.

The couple realized that the creature was a Bigfoot. Intrigued, they decided to leave it scraps of vegetables, which they did on a regular basis. Incredibly, the vegetables always disappeared. Then, one evening they didn't leave out any food. Later that night, the Bigfoot came and was apparently angry, as it took one of their garbage cans and threw it against the house. Hearing the noise, the husband grabbed his gun and ran outside. The Bigfoot stood only a few feet away. Frightened, the man shot his gun over the Bigfoot's head. The Bigfoot stared back unafraid. This time the husband fired a direct shot at the creature. Only then did it turn and run away. The Bigfoot never returned, and the couple learned the hard way that it's not always a good idea to feed wild animals, especially Bigfoot.

With footprints, handprints, and now butt-prints, what else is left? In September 2000 the **Bigfoot Field Researchers Organization** (BFRO) organized a 10-person expedition to Skookum Meadows, in the Cascade Mountains of southern Washington, and also the location of many Bigfoot encounters. The purpose of the expedition was to locate and obtain any evidence including tracks, hair, scat, signs of foraging, vocalizations, and hopefully even sightings. Unfortunately, there were no firsthand sightings, but what happened was even more unusual.

The team heard several vocalizations during the night and also found several sets of large tracks. They had set out a pile of fruit in the center of a large mud puddle hoping to attract a Bigfoot. When they went to examine the fruit, they were shocked to see that it was gone. Little bits of the fruit were scattered around. Most of it appeared to have been eaten by some creature.

As the team investigated a strange imprint left in the mud puddle, they were shocked at what they found. The tracks showed that a creature had apparently lain down in the mud to grab the fruit, leaving a near perfect imprint of its entire body. Jeff Meldrum wrote, "The depression appeared to be the imprint of a large hairy animal, as patterns of hair striations covered the various portions of the puzzling configuration. The three investigators considered what sort of animal could possibly be responsible for the impression. One by one, they eliminated the most likely potential candidates–deer, elk, bear, coyote–and eventually came to the realization that the only other large hairy animal remaining, with the bulk and requisite anatomy, was Sasquatch."

Casts were made of the imprint and examined by a panel of Bigfoot experts including Dr. John Bindernagel, Dr. Grover Krantz, Dr. Ron Brown, Jeff Meldrum, and others. According to Meldrum, "The unanimous consensus was that this could very well be the body imprint of a Sasquatch."

Most impressive were the dermatoglyphics found in parts of the imprint. Meldrum explained, "It appeared that the heel bore skin ridge detail . . . Consultations over the apparent dermatoglyphics, or skin ridges, were had with latent fingerprint examiner, Officer Jimmy Chilcutt. He found them to be consistent in texture and appearance with other specimens of purported Sasquatch tracks exhibiting such skin ridge detail."

Even more exciting, there were several suspicious hairs collected from the site. Examination of these hairs proved to be very interesting. Dr. Sarmiento, a primatologist, examined the hairs and concluded that they were from some type of unknown primate. Meldrum wrote, "A number of the hairs could not be readily identified, although they closely resemble primate hair in many characteristics. These hairs are very similar to an assemblage of independently collected hair samples curated by Dr. Henner Fahrenbach that are suspected of belonging to Sasquatch."[5]

The Skookum Meadows evidence, though not conclusive, remains intriguing.

BIGFOOT HAIR

One of the most famous things about Bigfoot is the fact that it is covered from head to toe with thick hair, except for the soles of the feet and the palms of the hands and (depending on the case) the facial area. The importance of hair to Bigfoot is clear because there are absolutely no cases of a completely *hairless* Bigfoot. With so many hairy beasts allegedly roaming through the forests, it is unavoidable that they would leave behind hair samples. In fact, there are dozens of such cases, and the hair samples are being studied by a special kind of scientist known as a trichologist. The study of hair identification, **trichology**, has proved to be an important part of Sasquatch science.

After the August 1958 Bluff Creek incident, several trichologists were given samples of hair and were told it was from a Sasquatch. Investigators, however, quickly ran into a problem. How could they tell if the hair was from a Sasquatch if they didn't know what Sasquatch hair actually looked like? Grover Krantz wrote, "The only way to positively identify a Sasquatch hair is to match it with a *known* sample."

Dr. F. Martin Duncan, who was in charge of the London Zoo's extensive hair collection, examined the Bluff Creek samples and was unable to match the hairs with any known North American mammal. He concluded that the hairs appeared to share "common features" with known primates, and yet he was unable to match it to any of them.

In 1968 police science instructor Ray Pinker was sent alleged Sasquatch hairs collected in central Idaho. Pinker was chosen to study the hairs because he had a large collection of hair samples from various animals. He was impressed by the sample. It did not match any known animal, but seemed to be a cross between a primate hair and a human hair. Like primates, the hairs showed variations in color and thickness and lacked a medullary core, and yet like humans, they had a familiar scale pattern. The scale pattern is a feature present in all human hair that allows trichologists to identify the hair as human. The medullary core is a soft, spongy substance in the center of human hair, except not in primate hair, which is another method trichologists can use to tell the difference between human and primate hair.

Several other scientists have studied samples of Sasquatch hair. Researcher Bob Titmus obtained a sample that he gave to Walter Birkby at the University of Arizona. Birkby studied the hairs and concluded that they were from a higher primate, but he was unable to match it with any known species.

In April 1976 a wave of sightings hit Flintville, Tennessee. After one particularly dramatic encounter in which a Bigfoot nearly abducted a small child, six men tracked the Bigfoot into a dense area of the forest, where they shot at it repeatedly. Later they found footprints and hair samples that were sent for scientific analysis. The results came back as "could not be identified."

Other scientists who have studied alleged Sasquatch hairs have encountered similar difficulties. In 1988 biochemist Jerold Lowenstein was sent Sasquatch hair samples to study. Lowenstein observed that the protein structure of the hairs was unique, though it appeared to be similar to humans and African apes.

In 1993 samples were obtained from a northern California case and examined by Sterling Bunnell, M.D., of the California Academy of Sciences. Dr. Bunnell wrote, "I have examined the hair specimen you provided from Damnation Creek and compared it by light microscopy under direct and transmitted illumination with human, chimpanzee, gorilla, orangutan and monkey hair. It is clearly related to the human-chimpanzee-gorilla group, but it is distinguishable from each of these."

In 1998 scientists in Shanghai, China, obtained samples of hairs that were believed to come from a local wild-man. Most of the hair was found to belong to various known species. However, six of the hairs proved to be very similar to human hair and other primates, but were also chemically unique. Grover Krantz wrote, "These hairs reportedly contained only 16 amino acids instead of the normal mammalian 17, and their iron-to-zinc ratio was 50 times higher than human and seven times higher than in the primate sample."

Molecular biologist Brian Sykes, of Oxford University, was given a sample of Yeti hairs collected from a case in Bhutan, where witnesses found what appeared to be a Yeti nest. Sykes had examined many types of hair samples, and after a close study of the Yeti hair, was deeply puzzled. As he said in an interview with *Smithsonian Magazine*, "We normally wouldn't have any difficulty at all. It had all the hallmarks of good material. It's not human; it's not a bear, nor anything else that we have so far been able to identify."

Currently several researchers are holding small collections of various Sasquatch and Yeti hair samples. It is hoped that in the future scientists will be able to use these samples to establish a connection between creatures from different regions. As of yet, however, this has not been done.[6]

BLOOD SAMPLES

In 2003 a Mr. Mossbeck and his friends went camping at Snelgrove Lake, Ontario, Canada, a place where they had camped many times

(continues on page 96)

A Word or Two About Sasquatch Poo

There are many ways to study wild animals. Zoologists are often unable to study species directly, so instead they study the evidence the animals leave behind. This includes not only footprints and hair samples, but also dung samples. Although it is very rare, there are now several cases on record in which alleged Bigfoot feces has been found. In a few cases, these samples have been subjected to various degrees of scientific study. The study of dung (**scatology**) reveals much about a creature. Bigfoot researcher Jeff Meldrum wrote, "It is a significant form of sign that conveys revealing information about the identity of the animal, the location of its activities, its size and diet."

In October 1955 William Roe was hiking through the wilderness 80 miles west of Jasper in Alberta, Canada, and he came upon a hairy figure, six feet tall, that was eating leaves from a group of bushes. The figure looked, he said, "partly human and partly animal." It shouted a strange call, which Roe said was "a kind of whinny, half-laugh and half language," and then bounded away. Roe examined the area and found piles of scat in five different places. According to Roe, "Although I examined it thoroughly, I could find no hair or shells or bugs or insects, so I believe it was strictly a vegetarian."

In 1958 during the Willow Creek wave of sightings, researchers discovered more than one pile of suspicious looking poo. A photographer who took pictures of the sample said that the feces was of "absolutely monumental proportions," adding that "I can only describe it as [like those of] a two-ton bear with chronic constipation."

Ray Wallace also came upon a sample which he said looked like human droppings except they were closer to the size of those from a 1,200 pound horse.

One of the earliest scientific studies of Bigfoot scat occurred in 1970, during an expedition sponsored by Robert Morgan of Miami, Florida. When tracks, hair samples, and some "strange fecal matter" were found, the fecal matter was submitted for study to the Smithsonian Institution in

Washington, D.C. According to their preliminary report, the fecal matter closely resembled that of bears. Interestingly, they were unable to positively identify it as bear dung, and so it remained a mystery.

In 1973 during a rash of Florida skunk-ape sightings, the St. Petersburg, Florida, Yeti Research Society (now disbanded) investigated dozens of cases, including one that they found particularly puzzling. There had been a number of sightings of the creature in a particular swampy area along the northwest Florida coastline. Upon researching the location, members were amazed to find a crude shelter made from interwoven tree branches. At first the structure seemed to be human-made, except there were no signs of human use. They did, however, find several 18-inch-long footprints and also, some suspicious-looking fecal matter which was allegedly "neither that of a human or any animal."

Researcher Bob Titmus has also studied several samples and says the Sasquatch scat almost always contains pine needles.

According to Grover Krantz, "There are many reports of fecal deposits that resemble those of humans, but which are said to have the volume of as much as an ordinary bucket–ten quarts. In some cases samples have been brought back for analysis, though only a few scientists are willing to look at such material when they are told its suspected source."

Dr. Vaughn Bryant, an anthropologist at Texas A&M University, studied two alleged samples. After examining them microscopically, Bryant was able to rule out humans, moose, elk, deer, and bear. While he was unable to identify the scat, he admitted that he still could not positively identify it as coming from a Sasquatch.

One of the most revealing studies was done by Dr. W. C. Osman Hill, of the London Zoological Society. The results were astonishing. Researcher Ivan Sanderson wrote, "This specimen shook up the scientists...this fecal mass did not in anyway resemble that of a known North American animal. On the other hand, it did look humanoid, but it had some peculiar features, as if the lower bowel had a spiral twist. But above all, it was composed exclusively of vegetable matter, and this, as far as could be identified, of

(continues)

(continued)

local fresh-water plants." The most exciting revelation, however, was that it contained a certain rare type of larval parasite which is not normally found in the feces of humans or the animals in the area.

One evening in September 1970, Jim Fielder, a biology teacher, drove along State Route 12 when he saw a reddish-brown, hairy figure crouching in the middle of the road. As he approached the figure jumped up on two legs and ran off into the woods. He knew instantly that he was seeing a Sasquatch. Fielder stopped his car and examined the area of the road where the creature had been crouching. He was shocked to see a "steaming wet spot in the road, three to four feet wide" where the animal had apparently urinated. Fielder said, "I was eager to get a sample, but I was dressed lightly and had no equipment with me."

Unfortunately, the sample was lost.

(continued from page 93)

before. They were in a very remote area, reachable only by plane, so they knew there wasn't anybody else in the forest. On this particular trip, something strange happened. Late at night, they heard the sound of something banging sticks together outside their cabin. Curious, they decided to respond to the weird knockings by knocking back. They took two sticks and banged them together loudly. At first nothing seemed to happen, but later that night, some type of very large creature attacked their cabin, physically shaking it. The creature outside roared loudly and then left. The next morning, the men found no evidence. A few months later when they returned to the cabin, they found it nearly destroyed. Suspecting that a Sasquatch might be responsible, they decided to videotape the damage and investigate this possibility.

Dr. Lynn Rogers is a wildlife biologist. He examined the videotape of the damage caused to the cabin and concluded that a bear did not do it. First of all, it was in the wintertime, when bears hibernate. Nor were there any claw marks. As he said, "I really am baffled by what did this."

The owner of the cabin, Mr. Mossbeck, decided to set out a bed of nails in front of the cabin doorway. He had previously used this device to deter bears from entering the cabin when he was gone. Three days after setting it out, the cabin was ransacked again, apparently by the same mysterious creature. The bed of nails didn't work as a deterrent, but when Mossbeck and his friends examined it, they were shocked to see a bloodstain along the edge of the board. Even more curious, it was in the shape of a giant footprint.

Investigators decided to stake out the cabin, and to their surprise, the Bigfoot returned. Although nobody saw it, some creature in the woods started throwing stones at the cabin.

Later, biologists examined the board and were able to retrieve not only blood samples, but also apparent tissue samples. These were given to Todd Disotell, professor of **anthropology** at New York University. Using the university's microbiology lab, Disotell analyzed the samples, looking for the **DNA** sequence in the hopes that they might be able to match it to a known species. Unfortunately, the samples appeared to be contaminated and could not be tested without first being separated from other substances.

Dr. Kurt Nelson at New York University knew how to do this. He was able to purify the sample and retrieve the DNA sequence. The results were nothing less than shocking. Said Nelson, "I found that it was identical to human DNA except that it had one nucleotide polymorphism. That nucleotide that is different is a difference that is shared with chimpanzees. I got DNA that was primate DNA, and I knew that I might be looking at the DNA of a Sasquatch."

Each creature on earth has unique DNA (deoxyribonucleic acid) in their cells. DNA is the genetic code that determines what type of creature an organism will become. Great apes share nearly identical DNA to humans, with only 35 genetic base pair deviations. Chimpanzees share 99 percent of their DNA with humans. The Snelgrove sample had only one genetic deviation. In other words, the results showed that the blood came from a primate somewhere between human and ape.

A hair sample retrieved from the board was examined by a scientist who said, "I looked at the hair under a microscope and compared it to every other North American mammal, especially the ones that live in Northern Ontario and it didn't match with anything, and is certainly not bear. It looked human to me, but there are two important differences in the morphology. One is that under a microscope there was no medulla. The other was that it had a naturally worn tip, a tapered tip. This had not been cut. It's almost like it came from a wild human. That left me confused about what it could be."

The Snelgrove case remains some of the best physical evidence for the existence of Bigfoot.[7]

The Unbelievable Cases

In 1871 a 17-year-old Native American girl was outside her home near Harrison Lake, in British Columbia. Suddenly, a Sasquatch appeared and, without warning, ran up to her, picked her up, and ran away. The young girl says the creature carried her for several miles, then forced her to swim across the Harrison River to a small rock shelter in the remote wilderness. In the shelter there were two other older Sasquatch, apparently the younger one's parents. The girl says that she was forced to stay with the Bigfoot family for one year, but was finally returned to her tribal homestead because she "aggravated [the Sasquatch] too much."

This story may sound incredible, but it is not unique. When it comes to Bigfoot, things can get very strange. There are several similar reports of Bigfoot kidnappings. The Native Americans have long known that the creatures sometimes attempt to capture humans. Researcher Jeff Meldrum wrote that several western Native American tribes have related to him traditional accounts of "crying children being snatched from under the wall of the teepees."

In 1924 Albert Ostman was on vacation at Toba Inlet, British Columbia, not far from the location of the above case. He decided to go camping and do some amateur gold prospecting at a mine in the area. He hired a Native American guide who agreed to take him, but warned him that the location was a known habitat of "the wild-man of the woods."

Ostman had never heard of such things and decided to take his chances. He brought three weeks of supplies with him. His guide took him to the location and quickly left. Ostman set up camp and went to bed. The next morning he was surprised to find that somebody or something had disturbed his supplies. He assumed it was an animal. The next night the strange visitor came again and disturbed his campsite. In the morning some of his food items were missing.

On the third night he attempted to stay awake to surprise the creature, but fell asleep. Sometime in the middle of the night he woke up to find himself being shoved inside his sleeping bag and carried like a sack of potatoes. He claims that he was unable to free himself and was carried for an estimated 30 miles before being let out of his sleeping bag.

Once set free, he was shocked to see that his kidnappers were four Bigfoot, two large ones (a male and a female) and two smaller ones (also male and female.) The large male who had kidnapped Ostman spoke in weird gibberish to the large female, who seemed very angry. The other two small ones appeared to Ostman to be afraid of him. They were all covered with thick brown hair except for the soles of their hands and feet, which had thick dark pads.

Ostman realized he was in a tiny hidden steep canyon. The home of the Bigfoot was nestled underneath a large rock overhanging, beneath which was a soft bed of moss and grasses where they slept. They also had made what looked like primitive blankets out of strips of bark that they wove together.

On the second day Ostman made his first attempt to escape. He ran toward the canyon edge, but the large Bigfoot, who was about eight feet tall, jumped up, blocked his way, and pushed him back, shouting at him the strange words, "Sooka-sooka!" Each of Ostman's other attempts to escape ended with the same result.

Over the next seven days he was forced to live with the Bigfoot. The older female and the young male left regularly to gather vegetables, roots, and nuts, which they placed in neat piles, offering small portions to Ostman.

Figure 7.1   *Some Bigfoot encounters include descriptions of Bigfoot families.*
(Fortean Picture Library)

He had some of his supplies with him, and these proved to be his method of escape. He had a package of snuff tobacco, which seemed to interest the Bigfoot. He finally gave it to the creature, who took the entire box and swallowed the contents. Moments later, the creature began to screech loudly, then grabbed a can of coffee grounds and poured them into his mouth. This caused the Bigfoot extreme distress, and he dashed away to get some water. Ostman took this rare opportunity and quickly grabbed a few supplies and ran away from the camp. The older female Bigfoot tried to stop him, but he managed to scare her and make his escape. He kept on the move until he made it back to civilization.

At first he told nobody his story. It wasn't until years later, when he heard that other people also had encountered Bigfoot that he revealed what happened. Ostman's skeptics have pointed out the fantastic nature of his story, and the fact that he had no evidence to back it up. However, several researchers including Grover Krantz and Ivan T. Sanderson interviewed Ostman before his death and came away convinced that his story is genuine. They pointed out that, despite the lack of any physical evidence to support them, the details reported by Ostman are consistent with other accounts, and that Ostman's story, while fantastic, is not unique.

One of the most dramatic accounts of a kidnapping occurred in 1928 on the west coast of Vancouver Island, on the west coast of Canada. Muchalat Harry was a member of the Nootka Tribe of Native Americans. He was an expert trapper and spent many weeks alone in the forests. One night he was sleeping in a campsite in one of his favorite hunting areas when, without any warning, he was picked up by a huge male Bigfoot and carried off several miles into the mountains.

When the morning light came, he found he was in a crude shelter beneath a rock shelf. Surrounding him were about 20 Bigfoot of all shapes sizes and colors. The older, larger males were in the front row. Behind them stood the older females. The youngest and smallest remained in the rear.

Although Harry was terrified, the creatures did not harm him. Instead, they pulled and poked at his full-length, woolen long underwear, seeming to think it was his skin or hair. This went on for a few hours, until by late afternoon the Bigfoot seemed to lose interest in him. When a large group of them left to go hunting and gathering, Harry leapt to his feet and ran for his life. He didn't look back to see if he was being chased, and instead ran and walked 12 miles out of the wilderness before reaching his tribal hometown of Nootka. He was badly scared by the incident and had to be convinced to reveal what happened. He refused to ever set foot in the area again.

Yet another kidnapping case occurred in 1940 in the Siskiyou Mountains of northern California. Two friends, O. R. Edwards and Bill Cole, were hunting when they saw an ape-like creature dart out of the woods, look at them, and dart back in. Next they heard the sound of something large running toward them through the forest, and Cole was attacked. Edwards said, "I heard the pad-pad-pad of running feet and the whump and grunt as their bodies came together. Dashing back to the end of the bush I saw a large manlike creature covered with brown hair. It was about seven feet tall and it was carrying in its arms what looked like a man. I could only see the legs and shoes."

Edwards looked to his side and saw that Cole was gone. The Bigfoot, he realized, had just kidnapped his friend.

Cole reports that he had no warning and suddenly found himself being carried through the forest by the creature, which held him tightly for a short time, then dropped him and sent him rolling down the hill.

The two men kept their encounter secret for years before finally revealing the event. Cole said, "Funny, neither of us had the guts to say what happened to us."[1]

The above kidnapping cases are extreme and lack physical evidence. However, on the other hand, they are remarkably consistent. If true, they reveal some surprising secrets about ape-men. It is well known that humans want to capture a Bigfoot. Now it seems clear that sometimes

Bigfoot want to capture humans. These cases also show that Bigfoot may be intelligent enough to have some type of language, the ability to hunt and gather food, construct crude shelters, and weave blankets from bark strips.

While Bigfoot kidnappings might seem scary, few of the victims claim to have been harmed or mistreated. Some Bigfoot encounters reveal a friendlier side of the furry creature, and in a few rare instances, people claim to have actually been rescued by Bigfoot.

FRIENDLY BIGFOOT

One summer evening in 1897, a young Native American male was walking home after fishing near in Tulelake, California, when he suddenly smelled a strong, musky odor. Looking up, he saw a large Bigfoot staring at him and grunting. The man gently laid down his fish, offering it as a gift toward the creature, and stepped back. The Bigfoot slowly approached and took the fish, then moved back into the trees, making a long, low howl.

Early one morning a few weeks later, the man again heard the Bigfoot stomping and whistling outside his cabin. On his doorstep he found a pile of fresh deerskins. As he picked up the skins, the Bigfoot howled in response in the forest. Over the next weeks and months, the Bigfoot brought other gifts, including fruits, berries and firewood.

The two creatures–man and Bigfoot–developed a friendship. This was good news for the young man three years later. In 1900 the man was exploring the slopes of Mount Shasta when a poisonous snake bit him. He killed the snake and fainted. Unfortunately he was miles away from civilization and was very sick. When he woke up he was surrounded by three Bigfoot, ranging in height from eight to 10 feet. They treated his wound and carried him back to a location where he was able to call for help.

The above case may seem unbelievable, but it is not unique. There are several reports of people who have been rescued by Bigfoot. In 1950 a logger from Ontonagon County, Michigan, had been pinned by a tree that fell on him in the wilderness. The man was knocked unconscious by the impact. When he woke up he was shocked to see that he was being rescued by two Bigfoot. One of the creatures lifted the tree while the other creature dragged him free. Once the logger was free, the Bigfoot set him down. Both the creatures then turned and walked back into the forest.[2]

BIGFOOT AND YETI CAPTURES

On July 3, 1884, a train traveled through the Canadian wilderness in British Columbia. Unknown to its passengers, numerous reports of a strange creature had been recently reported in the area. The train's engineer suddenly noticed a strange figure lying asleep besides the tracks. He blew the train's whistle and stopped the train. The passengers peered out the windows to see a short, hairy, man-like creature. As the train stopped, the creature leapt up and attempted to run away.

Several men on the train jumped off and gave chase. They managed to capture the creature 20 minutes later, which they dragged back to the train on a leash. The creature was quickly nicknamed "Jacko." He was 4 feet, 7 inches tall and weighed 127 pounds. One reporter wrote, "He has long, black, strong hair and resembles a human being with one exception: his entire body, except his hands (or paws) and feet are covered with glossy hair about one inch long. His forearm is much longer than a man's forearm, and he possesses extraordinary strength."

The creature didn't speak, but instead barked and growled. The passengers fed it milk and fruit, which it ate. One of the gentlemen on the train, Mr. George Telbury, took possession of the creature with the promise to exhibit him in London, England. There the story ends. Several researchers have attempted unsuccessfully to follow-up on the case. All traces of Jacko, unfortunately, have mysteriously disappeared.

Other stories of captured Bigfoot are similarly tantalizing. In 1902 the first telegraph line was built between Tibet and India. To complete the project, the telegraph cable had to be strung over the remote mountain passes between the two countries. The project was halfway finished when a problem developed. A group of workers (all local natives) failed to return to camp one evening, so a group of British soldiers was sent out to search for them. For some unknown reason, the workers had fled the area and couldn't be found. While checking the work site, however, the soldiers came upon an incredible sight: sleeping underneath a rock ledge, they observed a 10-foot-tall, human-like figure whose entire body was covered with hair except for the face. The creature reportedly had "long yellow fangs." The soldiers opened fire upon the strange ape-man, shooting it to death. They carried its body back to camp, packed it in ice and shipped it back to England to a British political officer named Sir Charles Bell. Unfortunately, there are no further reports of the creature after that. Numerous researchers have tried to follow-up on the story, but none have been able to verify the events.

Another case involves an alleged Yeti capture. In 1939 numerous Yeti encounters had occurred in a certain area of the Himalayas. The strange activity was disturbing the local inhabitants, so they decided to take action. They left out a bottle of liquor where the creature had been seen in the hopes that it would drink the alcohol and become drunk. The plan worked. The Yeti drank the liquor and was unable to defend itself as the residents tied it up. Unfortunately, the effects of the alcohol quickly wore off and the creature broke its bonds and escaped.

Stories of the captures of ape-men are not unique, but every case seems to lead to a dead-end. Still, the reports are intriguing. If somebody were to capture or kill a Yeti or Bigfoot it would provide the ultimate proof: an actual specimen. Until then, some researchers feel that no matter how many films are taken, or footprints measured, or hair samples gathered, the existence of the creature will remain unproven.[3]

PSYCHIC SHAPE-SHIFTING SASQUATCH

Wendy Collins (a pseudonym) claims she had her first encounter with a Bigfoot in 1997. She lived in the town of Acton, along the edge of

Bigfoot Children

It was early morning in October of 1975 and Bob Moody, a professional animal trapper from Alberta, Canada, was driving near his home when he saw three Sasquatch. One was about eight feet tall, but the other two were only four feet high. They were about 30 yards away, standing by the edge of the forest along the roadside. Moody suddenly realized he was seeing two Bigfoot kids standing next to their mother. According to Moody, "She was crouched, but when she heard the motor, she reared back. I began to pull the truck over but she and the smaller one disappeared. The whole thing happened in a matter of seconds." Later, when researchers investigated the location of the sighting, they found large and small footprints.

In 1976 Heide Ballard was picking blackberries near her home in Saddle Mountain State Park near Astoria, Oregon, where there had been several recent reports of Bigfoot. She happened to look up and saw something she will never forget. Ballard said, "I saw something which I feel sure was a baby Bigfoot...I saw a strange little creature sitting in a crotch of a tree. It was unlike anything I had ever seen, and about the size of my two-year-old. Its body was covered with light buff or beige-colored hair. Its hands and ears were like a human child. It had no tail. It was pulling blackberry vines towards it, and stuffing the berries in its mouth. I must have made a noise because it heard me and began to whimper."

Stunned, Ballard ran home to get her husband. When they returned to the location a few moments later, the baby Bigfoot was already gone.

Perhaps one of the most unbelievable stories of a young Bigfoot comes from Mount Shasta resident, Bonnie Feldman. In 1962 Feldman went out onto the porch of her trailer on the eastern slopes of Mount Shasta and was amazed to see a pregnant female Sasquatch lying down on the hillside above her home. As she watched, the Sasquatch gave birth to another baby Sasquatch. Feldman is apparently the only person to have witnessed this rare event.

the Angeles Crest forest outside of Los Angeles, California. She was having a vivid dream about Bigfoot one evening, then she woke up to actually see the creature. "I looked up outside of my window, and I saw the Bigfoot. I think he was about 9 feet tall, dark brown, hairy. And I could hear it growling outside my window."

The next morning her houseguest then told her that he too had dreamed about and seen the Bigfoot outside his bedroom window. They both ran outside and were shocked to see a line of very large footprints leading around the house. According to Collins, "Yes, there were footprints. You could see where he actually had to tiptoe past the dogs, and he would go up on his toes and he was so heavy that you could see where his toes would curl around the earth to balance him and sustain his weight."

Collins and her houseguest were amazed, however, this turned out to be just the beginning. Over the next few weeks, she not only had further encounters, she began to hear the Bigfoot talking to her telepathically. The message from the Bigfoot was always the same: "Come outside."

The Bigfoot was back two weeks later. Collins said, "I actually heard low growls around the yard first. I went outside. The horses were screaming like there was maybe a mountain lion or something outside. So I came outside to see why they were all screaming. And not only my horses were screaming, but all the surrounding horses were screaming like they were really, really freaked out and spooked. So I didn't know, maybe there were coyotes trying to take them down, or a mountain lion or a bear or something, because they were really freaked out. My neighbors got up and turned on their lights and checked their horses. And then everything settled down and everybody went back to bed. I was lying in my bed and I heard that weird 'Rrrrraaaahhhhhh-HHHHHH!' screaming down all through the wash. It sounded like a woman being murdered down in the wash."

On this occasion she didn't see the creature, but she could definitely smell it. Collins said, "He smells like dirty feet and stinky tennis shoes and rotting dead animal. He smells like a dumpster at high noon. It's really an odd smell. It smells like feces and manure and rotting flesh."

Collins not only heard and smelled the Bigfoot, but once again it began to communicate telepathically. According to Collins, "He would always talk to me and coax me. I could hear him in my mind. And he always tells me, 'Come outside. Come outside. I want to talk to you. Come outside.' And I'd say, 'I'm scared, I'm scared. I don't want to come outside. It's the middle of the night.' And he said, 'Face your fears, come outside.' Collins said he was very frightening for some reason, but at the same he was "intriguing. He's charismatic somehow. He's got a sense of allure, mystery, and a lot of fear."

Not surprisingly, Collins wondered if she was losing her mind. She knew the Bigfoot was real, but was she really in telepathic contact with it? She wasn't sure. "Well it was talking to me and telling me a lot about it, different things about their species and stuff. And he says, 'To prove that we're talking, I'll leave you a gift, I'll leave you a present on your porch. When you wake up in the morning, go out and get it.' I was like, okay, whatever, I'm just talking to myself anyway. I'll just flatter myself and go with it. So when I woke up the next morning I ran out to the front porch, and there, laying on the porch in all its glory, was this big, nasty spine with tendon-looking things hanging from it. And I was astounded. I've been talking to Bigfoot and he told me he was going to give me a gift and lo and behold, what does he give me, a spine." Unfortunately, the sample was lost before it could be studied.

The Bigfoot would always come at night. Often it would creep around the house, emitting long low growls. One evening, Collins smelled the creature outside as it telepathically tried to convince her to come outside. She refused. Shortly later she heard a loud clunk on the roof. The next morning she found a small boulder on top of the roof. The Bigfoot had thrown it up there. The boulder was so large it took two full-grown men to lift it down.

The encounters continued for the next few years. She never saw the creature, but could often sense its presence. Then one evening in 2003 her son, who was about five years old, started screaming in his bedroom. He called, "Mom, come quick! Come quick! The big hairy monkey man's in the tree! He's in the tree! Come, he's bending the tree over."

Collins went to her son's room, but by then the Bigfoot was gone. When she examined the tree the next day, she was surprised to see that it had been badly damaged. "The whole top of the tree was bent over in half."

The encounters came to a climax one evening when the Bigfoot again tried to telepathically convince Collins to come outside at night and meet him face-to-face. According to Collins, "He kept trying to get me to come outside and talk to him, come outside and talk to him. And I just said, 'Look, I can hear you. Just talk to me. I can hear you from right here.' And he said, 'No, I need you to come outside.' I said, 'I just can't bring myself. You scare me. You really, really scare me. You're big, you're hairy, you're stinky, and I'm scared.' And he said, "Well, we can change shapes. We can change forms.' And I said, 'Well, is there any way you can take a form that's a little more pleasing to the eye. Because I'm really sorry, but I'm scared of you.' And he said, 'Yes, I can do that.'"

A few days after that incident, Collins was outside working with her horses. Suddenly, a giant dog came running up to her as if it had known her forever. "It was running right at me, just running, charging. And I panicked. I went to run inside. And something stopped me. I didn't; I just stayed perfectly still. And then it ran right up to me with its tail wagging. And I thought it was one of the most beautiful dogs I had ever seen. It looked kind of like a cross between a wolf and a husky. And immediately I fell in love with him. He had really strange yellow eyes. I had never really seen the Bigfoot's eyes. Anyway, I just fell in love with him, and I took him with me everywhere."

Collins tried to find his owners, but nobody seemed to know the dog. She felt compelled to care for him. It wasn't long before strange things began to happen. She'd lock the dog in the fence in the yard, and he'd appear in the house. She'd lock him in the house, and he'd magically appear outside.

Collins said, "It was so strange. It started getting really creepy. Like I'd put him in the house, and I'd come to the front and he'd be in the front. It was really, really odd. How the heck did he get out?"

Collins kept the dog for about two or three months. She had to leave her home to do errands one day and didn't want the dog to get away so she locked him in the house. Little did she know, she would never see the dog again, at least not in that form.

According to Collins, "I had to leave him in the house, and I took off to go do what I needed to do. And when I got back, he was gone. He was out of the house. I looked everywhere. He was just gone. I never saw him again. And I was absolutely broken-hearted because I just fell in love with this dog. So then one day I heard the Bigfoot, because I could hear him in my head many times. He said, 'How are you?' I said, 'I'm not doing so well right now. I had this dog that I just fell madly in love with. And he vanished. He's just gone and I'm really heartbroken about it.' He said, 'You really loved the dog?' And I said, 'I really did.' And he said, 'Was that form a little more pleasing to the eye?' And I just went, 'Oh my god! No way!!!' But he basically alluded to the fact that *that* was him. And he came in to show me that I could interact with him and love him and feel very attached to him. And he was in that animal form."

After about seven years, the Bigfoot stopped coming around. During that time, Collins brought in investigators, at least two of who claimed to have heard the Bigfoot either growling or tromping through the brush. None uncovered any hard evidence to confirm Collins' reports. As of 2005, Collins has had no further encounters. She has no idea why the Bigfoot chose her. She speculates that it was because she was somehow sensitive enough to hear it telepathically. The Sasquatch told her that they have the ability to shape-shift and turn invisible, and that many of them live in underground areas. She, of course, believes that they are intelligent and spiritual creatures, which should be protected not hunted.[4] In recent years other reports have surfaced involving invisible, shape-shifting, telepathic Bigfoot.

A similar case is that of Lunetta Woods of southern Wisconsin. On January 5, 1994, Woods was with her husband and two children in their farmhouse in the Wisconsin woods when her son shouted out that he saw strange tracks in the snow outside. Woods crept outside and saw what appeared at first to be deer tracks. However, as she followed the tracks they grew larger in size. Creeping further ahead, they transformed into what looked like giant, human footprints. As they went off into the woods, the tracks transformed back into deer tracks. Woods was mystified and wondered how the tracks could change like that.

Over the next few days and weeks, more strange tracks appeared. They too seemed to transform into the prints of different creatures including deer, rabbit, some kind of reptile, and enormous Bigfoot-type prints. When she measured the Bigfoot prints, they were 13 inches long with a 5½-foot stride. Woods had seen enough tracks of the local wildlife to see that these tracks were different and appeared to be typical Bigfoot tracks. She wondered if Bigfoot could be a shape-shifter.

Her suspicions seemed confirmed when she and her entire family began to dream about Bigfoot. They also began to smell the odor of Bigfoot at night, and even hear strange whistling noises. Woods' dreams became more intense as the Sasquatch came to her and explained that they were intelligent, spiritual creatures, and that they had the ability to shape-shift and turn invisible. They warned her that humans were damaging the earth's environment through pollution. They explained that Sasquatch are "earth keepers–healers and protectors of Mother Earth." Finally they told Woods that they wanted her to write a book about them, which she did. Her book, *Story in the Snow*, recounts her encounters from the point of view of Sasquatch, but offers no hard evidence to support her claims. According to Woods, "There are other people outside of my family who have had Sasquatch experiences . . . I have been guided through dreams to keep a low profile about my relationship with Bigfoot, only sharing my story with those whom I feel are spiritually rich." Despite wanting to keep a low profile, Woods decided to write her book because she felt her experiences were too important to keep to herself.[5]

These reports of telepathic, shape-shifting creatures echo certain elements common in accounts of contact with extraterrestrials, which sometimes involve similar messages warning of the need to protect the earth. Perhaps even more baffling, though, are reports in which UFOs and Bigfoot appear together.

BIGFOOT AND UFOS

In 1981 a Rome, Ohio, family that has chosen to remain anonymous discovered very strange footprints outside their farmhouse. The prints were three-toed, 14 inches long, and 1½-inches deep. Soon, several members of the family saw who was making the footprints. They first noticed something was wrong when they smelled a strong, unpleasant odor. Then, looking to the woods, they saw hairy gorilla-like creatures that were nine feet tall and had hairless faces and long fangs. Around this time, the family began to lose many of their ducks and chickens to the creatures. On one occasion, a large "UFO-like thing" flew over the house. The witnesses tried shooting at the object, but the gun had no effect. They also tried to shoot at the Bigfoot, but whenever they appeared, they stayed at the edge of the woods and then disappeared.

In 1978 radiologist Robert Murphy was home in Canyon Country, California, one evening when a flash of light coming from the backyard caught his eye. Looking outside he was shocked to see what appeared to be a UFO landing in the corner of his backyard. According to Murphy, "There were red and white lights flashing, and they looked like they were on an object."

At first he thought it might be a helicopter, but there was no sound. After a few moments, the object disappeared. At first, the encounter seemed over. But the very next night Murphy had an even stranger experience. In the very same location that he saw the UFO, he heard a loud creature start to growl. At the same time all his dogs started to bark. Murphy was convinced he was hearing Bigfoot. "I heard this thing, this creature. And this thing moaned in an unearthly fashion that's very hard to describe . . . it sounded like it was resonating in a

Figure 7.2 *In 1978 a UFO allegedly landed in the backyard of radiologist Robert Murphy in Canyon Country, California. The next day, he had an encounter with a Sasquatch. In some rare cases, it appears Sasquatch and UFOs are related.* (Kesara Art)

very large creature . . . I thought it was Bigfoot." The next morning, he found strange footprints in the area.

A third incident occurred on December 4, 1970 and was reported by the Bowers family of Vader, Washington. It was snowing and when the family went outside, they found a track of footprints, each measuring 16 inches long, 6 inches wide, and 1½ inches deep. The family was visited by a UFO three days later. It was early morning when a "bright star" moved across the sky and then closer to the witnesses. They saw that it was a dome-shaped object with an outer rim. It glowed bright orange and then moved away.

While more cases of psychic, telepathic, or UFO-related Sasquatch encounters have been reported, many investigators shy away from these reports and are at a loss to explain them. Some theorize that there may be different kinds of Sasquatch, one that is a physical animal, and another "para-ape" with psychic abilities. A few even speculate that some Bigfoot may be extraterrestrial. Unfortunately there is little evidence to support these theories. Such cases are very few in number and comprise probably less than 1 percent of the number of Bigfoot reports. Yet, to solve any mystery, all of the evidence must be considered. Until somebody can explain the psychic, telepathic, and UFO aspects of these rare Sasquatch encounters, the mystery will remain unsolved.[6]

Famous Hoaxes

On May 15, 1977, at 8:30 a.m., Pat Lundquist, a bus driver for Pacific State Lines Bus, stopped his bus to pick up a passenger. He then resumed his journey along the heavily forested Lougheed Highway toward the city of Mission in British Columbia, Canada.

Not far ahead of him on the highway, he was startled to observe a large, hairy, man-like creature, walking on two legs, step out from behind the trees and walk across the road. Lundquist slammed on the brakes and brought the bus to a stop.

"Look at the Sasquatch!" he shouted to his passengers.

Jumping up, several passengers also saw the Bigfoot cross the road and disappear into the trees. Lundquist dashed out of the bus and actually chased the creature into the forest. The creature quickly disappeared, but Lundquist did find several footprints.

He returned to the bus and continued toward the city of Mission. He stopped at the next phone booth and made a police report. The police began an investigation and were able to locate the footprints. Meanwhile, somebody called radio stations, and before long the story became front-page news across Canada and the United States. Spectators began to arrive within hours of the incident. Over the next few days, more than a thousand visitors came to the site to gaze at the footprints.

Bigfoot experts also converged on the scene. Longtime researchers John Green, René Dahinden, and Dennis Gates had no trouble finding the site due to the enormous crowds. Their main worry was that the evidence would be destroyed. Instead, they found that the police had carefully staked off the area with yellow tape, preserving the footprints perfectly. The experts took their time to carefully measure the footprints. They were 14½-inches long with a stride-length of 5 feet. The prints were also 1½-inches deep, indicating that whatever made the tracks was very heavy. They photographed the scene and made plaster casts of the footprints. They also interviewed the witnesses. All the researchers were convinced that the witnesses were sincere.

At first the case seemed perfect. The researchers agreed that it had all the elements of a perfect case: numerous firsthand eyewitnesses and several clear-cut footprints. But as they began to carefully examine the evidence they collected, the story began to fall apart. John Green (an expert on animal tracks) was the first to voice his suspicions. When the researchers received enlargements of the photographs of the tracks, they were stunned. None of the telltale marks of genuine footprints were there. There was no dermal-ridge detail, no curvature, and most importantly, they were flat. It was obvious that the tracks were made by a rigid object applying vertical pressure only, with no weight shifting from heel-to-toe. In other words, they were fake.

Green and the others called the police and told them their conclusions. The police were shocked, especially because the witnesses refused to change their story. A few days later, however, the truth came out. After making a deal with the police that they wouldn't be prosecuted, four young men confessed that they had hoaxed the entire incident.

The four young men, Don Ticehurst (26), his brother Ken (24), René Quensel (19), and Gordon Jacobi (26) had planned the prank for weeks. They memorized the bus schedule. They picked a perfect site where they would enact the incident. They bought a gorilla costume and equipped everyone with walkie-talkies.

The day before the incident, they crept to the chosen location and carefully faked a set of footprints using large carved wooden feet. They made sure not to leave any of their own footprints at the site.

On the morning of the sighting, Ken Ticehurst, who was nearly six feet tall and weighed 165 pounds, put on the gorilla suit. The bus arrived right on schedule, and Ken walked across the road in front of it and disappeared into the forest. His friend, René, was waiting there to help him out of the costume and then hide.

The four young men returned to town. Don Ticehurst was the one who called the radio stations and leaked the story to the press. However, none of the young men were prepared for the explosive reaction. They became worried when the police came to investigate, followed by actual Bigfoot experts. Then came the front-page headlines and the hundreds of spectators. Fearing that things had gotten out of hand and that they might be in trouble with the law, the hoaxers agreed to confess. Said Don Ticehurst in his confession, "It was just a good practical joke. We thought it might fool a few people. We meant no harm, and committed no crime."[1]

While anyone can claim to see a Bigfoot, what many hoaxers don't realize is that Bigfoot researchers are often able to determine if a case is genuine or not by examining the evidence. Genuine cases contain many indicators pointing toward the reality of the event. On the other hand, hoaxed cases often contain inconsistencies that do not match the patterns that have been revealed in other cases. Using these methods, it becomes easy for the experienced investigator to recognize a hoax.

KIDNAPPED BY BIGFOOT?

In May 1976 several newspaper articles carried an incredible story told by Cherie Darvell of Redding, California. While hiking in the rugged mountain country, Darvell's friends told authorities that she became separated from them and was lost in the wilderness. A small army of sheriff's deputies, Forest Service employees, and volunteers began a days-long search for the young woman. After several days, Darvell emerged from the forest and told an incredible story. She claimed that she had been kidnapped and held captive by Bigfoot.

Figure 8.1 *One of a series of photos of an alleged Bigfoot in a swamp. Investigators first impressed by the photos concluded that the figure is probably a fake, possibly a model, when further examination showed that it remained in exactly the same position in each image.* (Fortean Picture Library)

Upon being questioned by authorities on the details, her story allegedly fell apart.

It seemed that Darvell and her friends had come to the area with
the intention of producing a Bigfoot film, and had concocted the entire story. Authorities quickly labeled the case a hoax. Whether true
or not, the days-long search for Darvell cost taxpayers an estimated
$11,513 dollars.[2]

A HAIRY HOAX

In 1987 several clumps of alleged Sasquatch hair were recovered from
the Blue Mountains of Oregon and given to numerous labs for study.
The initial investigations seemed promising as the hair appeared to
be human-like but with minor differences. Finally, a sample was given
to the Japan Hair Medical Science Lab where, after subjecting it to
various tests, researchers declared it to be "synthetic fiber." The fibers
were later positively identified as a product known as "Dynel," which is
often used to make imitation hair for wigs. Even after the fibers were
found to be fake, new samples continued to be found as late at 1991.
According to leading researcher Grover Krantz, "Clearly someone
was planting samples of Dynel fiber in many places in the Blue Mountains. . . . This ongoing fiasco only illustrates the problem we have of
sorting out the fake evidence from what may be real."[3]

A BIGFOOT NEST?

The Blue Mountains of Oregon had produced a steady stream of Bigfoot reports for many years, so when researcher Grover Krantz heard
that somebody had located an alleged Sasquatch nest, he raced to the
scene. He was amazed at what he found. Somebody or something had
torn dozens of inch-diameter branches from fir trees and laid them out
in random layers, forming a bed about 8 feet long and 4 feet wide—the
perfect size for a Sasquatch. Even more exciting, numerous hairs were
still clinging to the branches.

(continues on page 124)

No Bigfoot Hunting: It's the Law! Or is it?

While it's technically not illegal to hoax a Bigfoot encounter, it could be dangerous. There are many hunters who are hoping to kill a Bigfoot. Certainly, the first person to do so would be famous. He or she might also become *infamous*. If the Bigfoot turns out to be closer to human than to an animal, would this be considered murder? And if Bigfoot is just a rare animal, wouldn't it be considered an endangered species, and therefore protected by law?

Because mainstream science has not yet recognized Bigfoot as an official species, these questions are difficult to answer. Despite this, there have been several attempts to make it illegal to shoot a Bigfoot.

In 1975 researcher Peter Byrne contacted a senior official from the fish and wildlife branch of the Department of Recreation and Conservation in Victoria, British Columbia, a well-known Bigfoot hotspot, and inquired about the legalities involved in Bigfoot hunting. The official responded with the following answer: "Only those species of animals listed in our Game Regulations may be hunted or killed. Therefore, if such a creature as a Sasquatch were to be hunted or shot it would be illegal and, should the creature prove to be human, it would be murder."

In 1977 a unique bill was presented to the Oregon state legislature, which would make it illegal to harass or kill any Bigfoot. Within the year, the legislature received more than 1,000 letters from researchers, environmentalists and witnesses, urging them to support the bill. Despite this, the members of the legislature refused to take the issue seriously and even ridiculed the bill. One member put on a gorilla suit, alerted the media, and danced around in the suit in the House chambers. When the time came to present the bill, the hearings were jammed with spectators eager to see which way the vote would go. To many people's disappointment, the bill was quickly defeated.

Probably the most famous law concerning Bigfoot hunting comes from Skamania County in Washington State. After several local Bigfoot

encounters, on April 1, 1969, the Skamania County Board of Commis-
sioners passed Ordinance 69-01, which states:

> Be it hereby ordained by the Board of County Commissioners
> of Skamania County, whereas, there is evidence to indicate the pos-
> sible existence in Skamania County of a nocturnal primate mammal
> variously described as an ape-like creature or a sub-species of Homo
> Sapiens, and whereas, both legend and purported recent sightings
> and spoor support this possibility, and whereas, this creature is gener-
> ally and commonly known as Sasquatch, Yeti, Bigfoot or Giant Hairy
> Ape, and whereas, publicity attendant upon such real or imagined
> sightings has resulted in an influx of scientific investigators, as well as
> casual hunters, many armed with lethal weapons, and whereas, the
> absence of specific laws covering the taking of specimens encourages
> laxity in the use of firearms and other deadly devices and poses a clear
> and present threat to the safety and well-being of persons living or
> traveling within the boundaries of Skamania County as well as to the
> creatures themselves, therefore be it resolved that any premeditated,
> willful and wanton slaying of any such creature shall be deemed a felo-
> ny punishable by a fine not to exceed Ten Thousand Dollars ($10,000)
> and/or imprisonment in the county jail for a period not to exceed Five
> (5) years. Be it further resolved that the situation existing constitutes
> an emergency and as such this ordinance is effective immediately.

As of 2008 nobody has been charged for breaking the ordinance. Pioneering Bigfoot researcher Grover S. Krantz has pointed out that despite
the Skamania ordinance, until Bigfoot is accepted as an official species,
any laws pertaining to it are essentially meaningless. According to Krantz,
"In the state of Washington, for example, the Game Department does
not recognize the Sasquatch as an existing species. The head of their
legal division told me that officially they would take no notice even if a
hunter brought one in. They would formulate a policy only if and when
the scientists decided it was real."

(continued from page 121)

Krantz collected the hairs and sent them to be scientifically analyzed. Meanwhile, as he examined the site, he noticed something that bothered him. The location was only 50 yards from a well-traveled road. It seemed unlikely that a Sasquatch would build a bed that close to a road. Still, there were tracks in a nearby area that seemed to be genuine, and there were also reports of strange vocalizations at night.

When analysis of the hairs came back, Krantz had his answer. As he wrote, "[The nest] contained many of the hairlike strands that later turned out to be artificial fibers. These facts raise suspicions that suggest it was not legitimate."

Krantz was disappointed. It was another hoax. Hoaxes like this not only made his job more difficult, they polluted the legitimate evidence with false data. Because of this, he was unable to reach any solid conclusions regarding the Bigfoot nest. As he wrote, "We do know that fake hairs were planted at the site, but how much of the rest of it was real, if any, is not now determinable."[4]

A YETI SCALP?

In 1960-1961 famous Mount Everest climber Edmund Hillary went on an expedition to the Himalayas in Nepal to search for the Yeti. Although his team didn't encounter any Yeti, they did retrieve an alleged Yeti scalp, which they obtained from a sherpa. The scalp was said to be 240 years old. It was covered with short, dark, and coarse hair. The object was considered sacred by the sherpas. In 1961 the scalp was flown to London for scientific study. Scientists from three different countries concluded that the scalp was a fake. It was not from a Yeti, but rather from a rare goat-antelope found in the Himalayas called a *serow*.

Yeti scalps are considered sacred objects in the region, and there are rumors that several genuine artifacts are being held in various monasteries in Tibet. Another alleged Yeti scalp was obtained by Edmund Hillary, but scientific study again revealed it to be a fake. In this case, the artifact was made from the hide of the rare Tibetan blue bear.[5]

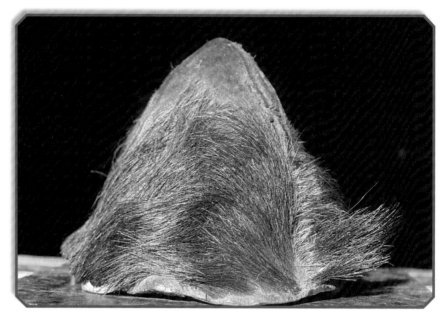

Figure 8.2 *An alleged Yeti scalp. Similar scalps have turned out to be fakes made from the hides of animals such as the serow, a rare goat-antelope.* (Christophe Boisvieux/Corbis)

HOAXES NOT COMMON

As with many fields of science, there are occasional hoaxes in crypto-zoology, but most experts do not believe that the hoax explanation can account for all the evidence. According to expert Dennis Gates, "For every false sighting, I can point to a thousand others which appear to be genuine. We have accumulated enough evidence to prove to our satisfaction beyond a doubt that Bigfoot or Sasquatch is real. There have been too many footprints found at hundreds of widely separated places. They couldn't all have been made by pranksters. Unfortunately, we have not yet gained the kind of hard evidence, such as a carcass or a skeleton, to prove to scientists that we are right. So searching for that evidence is what keeps us going."[6]

While a hoax might seem like a harmless prank, it can actually cause considerable damage. Hoaxes not only waste the time of Bigfoot researchers, but the false data pollutes the true data, leading to false conclusions. Also, hoaxes can make other people think that all cases involving Bigfoot or other cryptozoological creatures can be explained by hoaxes. This can be especially upsetting to firsthand witnesses who have actually encountered the creature and then find themselves victims of ridicule as possible hoaxers. Thankfully, as most experts agree, there are few apparent hoaxes in proportion to legitimate reports.

Today, Bigfoot and Yeti researchers continue to study the available evidence. While the hoax explanation fails to account for all of the Bigfoot evidence, conclusive evidence that the creatures are real remains elusive. And so the mystery continues.

Timeline

1818   First newspaper articles are published reporting Bigfoot encounters in New Jersey and New York.

1840   Missionary Elkanah Walker lives among the local Native Americans and writes about their belief that a "race of giants" live in the nearby mountains.

1850s   Two hunters encounter Bigfoot in Idaho, a story which is later recorded by President Theodore Roosevelt in his memoirs.

1868   Surveyor Charles Barrington Brown hears the howling of the wild ape-men said by the local natives to live in the jungles of British Guiana, in South America.

1871   A Native American woman claims to be kidnapped by a Bigfoot near British Harrison Lake, in British Columbia, Canada.

1884   A "half-man, half-beast" creature nicknamed Jacko is found and captured near Yale, British Columbia, Canada.

1886   Hunter Jack Dover encounters a Bigfoot in Happy Camp, California.

1887   Major Lawrence Waddell encounters apparent Yeti footprints in the Tibetan Himalayas.

1895   Major S. E. Ingraham claims to encounter a telepathic Bigfoot in a cave on the summit of Mount Rainier in Washington State.

1900   A Native American man is rescued by a friendly Bigfoot after being bitten by a snake in the wilderness of Mount Shasta, California.

1901   Lumberman Mike King encounters a Bigfoot on Vancouver Island in British Columbia, Canada.

1902 A group of British soldiers building a telegraph line through the Himalayas allegedly encounter and kill a Yeti.

1907 A group of Bigfoot terrorize an entire village in Bishops Cove, British Columbia, Canada.

1909 A Sasquatch nicknamed Old Yellow Top (because it has blond hair on the top of its head) makes its first of several appearances in Ontario, Canada.

1912 Surveyor Charles Harper encounters an ape-like creature on Currockbilly Mountain in New South Wales, Australia. He learns that the locals know about the creatures and call them Yowies.

1915 Explorer Henry J. Elwes publishes a report of ape-man sightings (including his own) in the foothills of the Himalayas. Three frontiersmen encounter an 8-foot-tall Bigfoot in British Columbia, Canada.

1921 Colonel C. K. Howard-Bury and others observe several Yeti and later find footprints in the Tibetan Himalayas.

1923 Members of a mountain climbing expedition on Mount Everest observe a large, hairy ape-man run across a snowfield.

1924 Camper Albert Ostman is kidnapped by a Bigfoot in British Columbia, Canada. A group of loggers working in the Cascade Mountains are attacked by several Bigfoot, who throw stones at them and chase them out of the area. Also, a group of miners in Ape Canyon near Mount St. Helens are attacked by several Bigfoot and forced to leave their cabin.

1925 Russian troops allegedly kill and bury a wild ape-man that they discover in the Pamir Mountains of Russia. Scientist A. N. Tombazzi observes a Yeti digging for roots with a stick in the Himalayan foothills.

1927 Tourists Cuthburt Burgoyne and his wife observe a bipedal ape-man walking among a group of baboons while traveling by boat up the coast of East Africa.

1930 A hunter named Inocencio is attacked by a wild ape-man in the jungles of Patagonia, in southern Argentina.

1936 Geographer Ronald Kaubatch finds a set of Yeti tracks at an elevation of 16,000 feet in the Himalayas of Nepal. Mountaineer

Eric Shipton encounters more Yeti tracks while traveling through Katmandu.

1937   Frontiersman Datus Perry has the first of many encounters with Sasquatch in the wilderness outside of Carson, Washington. Captain William Hichens reveals his encounter with two short, hairy ape-men while on a lion hunt in the jungles of East Africa.

1940   Hunter Bill Cole is picked up and carried by a Bigfoot while hunting with his friend in the Siskiyou Mountains of northern California.

1941   The Chapman family of Ruby Creek, British Columbia, Canada, are frightened out of their home by an aggressive Sasquatch. Lieutenant Colonel V. S. Karapetyan observes a wild-man that had been captured by the local natives in the mountain wilderness near Buinaksk, Russia.

1942   Slavomir Rawicz and others observe two large Bigfoot while hiking through the Himalayan Mountains.

1944   Three English explorers observe a Yeti run down a hillside in the wilderness of Kashmir.

1950   A logger from Ontonagon County in Michigan says that a tree fell on him, pinning him to the ground, and he was later rescued by two Bigfoot who lifted the tree off his body.

1951   English explorer Eric Shipton photographs 13-inch-long tracks on Mount Everest.

1952-1953   Sir Edmund Hillary launches expedition to Himalayas and locates hair samples and footprints.

1954   Film director Pai Hsin and others observe two Chinese ape-men in the Pamir Mountains of northern China.

1956   Geologist Audio Pich encounters a set of 17-inch tracks in the Andes Mountains of Argentina. Researcher John Keel follows Yeti tracks and later observes the creature in the Himayalas.

1957   Scientist A. G. Pronin observes a Yeti in the Pamir Mountains of Russia. A Yeti is killed after attacking a young woman in a small village in the Chinese province of Zhejiang. Bigfoot/Yeti hunter Tom Slick launches an expedition and locates hair samples and excrement in the Arun Valley. Some members observe the Yeti firsthand.

1958 Construction workers Wilbur Wallace, Jerry Crew, and others discover huge footprints around their work site outside of Bluff Creek, California. After equipment is found vandalized and others start seeing Bigfoot in the area, the story becomes widely publicized and the creature is given the name Bigfoot.

1959 Sherpa Da Tempa encounters a Yeti in the Arun Valley of the Himayalas. Tom Slick launches third Yeti hunt and locates more tracks.

1960 Native villagers of the jungles of southern Mexico and Guatemala report sightings of a "wild-man" which lives at the higher elevations. Around the same time, exotic animal dealer Claus U. Oheim hears reports of other wild ape-man coming from the jungles of Ecuador and Columbia. In Nyasaland, at Nkata Bay in Africa, game rangers receive numerous reports of a large shaggy creature. Upon investigating the area, they find more than 30 apparent ape-man nests.

1961 Explorer and mountain climber Edmund Hillary launches an expedition to the Himalayas in Nepal to search for the Yeti. They return from the expedition with what they believe is a genuine Yeti scalp retrieved from the local natives. Analysis shows the scalp to be from a rare type of goat-antelope called a serow.

1965 Two families, the Crabtrees and the Fords, of Fouke, Arkansas, encounter a large, hairy Sasquatch. When more neighbors began to report encounters, the events became widely publicized.

1967 Roger Patterson films a female Bigfoot at Bluff Creek, California. Some believe the film to be a hoax, while others call it the best evidence of Bigfoot to date.

1968 Researchers Ivan T. Sanderson and Bernard Heuvelman inspect an apparent frozen Yeti at a carnival sideshow in Chicago, Illinois. The body is fully encased in ice and appears to be covered from head to toe with hair. The owner claims that it is an actual captured Yeti. The researchers believe it to be genuine and give it the name, the Minnesota Iceman. They return at a later date for a closer inspection and find that the body has been switched for a fake. The owner refuses to say what happened to the original body or release any other information.

1969 Butcher Joe Rhodes of Bossburg, Washington, discovers a set of Sasquatch footprints in the area. Researchers investigate and locate another remarkable set of footprints apparently from the same creature, which due to a deformity on its foot, is given the name Old Cripple Foot. Officials in Skamania County, Washington, pass legal Ordinance 69-01, which makes it illegal to hunt or kill Bigfoot. Violators may be fined up to $10,000 dollars and receive five years imprisonment.

1970 Zhang Qilin of Xikiangli Village in China observes a Yeti stealing and eating corn from the crop-fields he is guarding. At the same time, a wave of Yeti sightings sweeps across the province. The Bowers family of Vader, Washington, find strange Bigfoot-like prints outside their home. Shortly later, they see a UFO move over their home.

1971 The Bigfoot Information Center (one of the first civilian Bigfoot research organizations, now defunct) is founded by Bigfoot researcher Peter Byrnes. Also, the Fouke Monster makes another appearance, in Fouke, Arkansas. A wave of sightings of the Florida Skunk-Ape sweeps across the state. When the sightings continue, the Florida Everglades earn a reputation for producing a large number of Skunk-Ape reports.

1972 Primatologist John Napier becomes the first scientist to publish a book about Sasquatch. Momo, the Missouri Monster, is seen by two children outside their home. Biologists Howard Cronin and Jeffrey McNeely observe a Yeti and its footprints in the Himayalas. The film *The Legend of Boggy Creek*, based on events in Fouke, Arkansas, is released and becomes an unexpected success.

1976 Old Yellow Top makes his final appearance in Ontario, Canada.

1977 The Chinese Academy of Sciences in Peking organizes a 110-member expedition to the Hubei Province where they discover many unusual footprints and hair samples.

1978 Radiologist Robert Murphy sees a UFO land in his backyard in Canyon Country, California. The very next night, he hears a

Bigfoot growl three times in the exact same area. He also finds footprints.

1979   Mountaineers John Edwards and John Allen discover an apparent Yeti nest and footprints in the Himalayas.

1980   A group of Chinese scientists discover at least 11 alleged Yeti nests in the Zhejiang Province of China.

1981   A family in Rome, Ohio, encounters Bigfoot-like creatures, while at the same time a large UFO flies over their home.

1982   The International Society of Cryptozoology (ISC) is founded.

1987   The movie *Harry and the Hendersons* is released, eventually earning more than $21 million in box-office sales.

1994   Lunetta Woods and her family encounter strange tracks outside their home in rural Wisconsin. Woods later claims to have telepathic contact with the creatures, who call themselves healers and protectors of Mother Earth.

1995   The Bigfoot Field Researchers Organization (BFRO) is founded by researcher Matt Moneymaker.

1997   Wendy Collins and her family and friends encounter a Bigfoot around their home in Acton, California. Collins later claims to have telepathic communication with the creature, which she believes can shape-shift.

2000   The BFRO organizes a 10-person expedition to Skookum Meadows in Washington State where they discover a full-body print of a Bigfoot. Bigfoot Museum opens in Willow Creek, California.

2003   A group of campers encounter Bigfoot at Snelgrove Lake, in Ontario, Canada. The Bigfoot later attacks their cabin. Scientists are able to retrieve and analyze DNA and blood samples that appear to be neither ape nor human, but a mixture of both.

Glossary

ABOMINABLE SNOWMAN   See Yeti

ANTHROPOLOGY   The study of humankind and human evolution

APE-MEN   Bipedal primates with half-human, half-ape appearance, and unrecognized as official species

BFRO   Bigfoot Field Researchers Organization, a leading civilian investigative group

BIGFOOT   An alleged large hairy primate seen in North America and unrecognized as an official species

CRYPTOZOOLOGY   The study of creatures unknown or unaccepted as official species

DERMATOGLYPHICS   Skin-ridge detail found on the palms and soles of primates, for example, a fingerprint

DNA   Deoxyribonucleic acid, the genetic code found in all living creatures; each species contains its own unique sequence of DNA

GIGANTOPITHECUS   The largest known ape to ever live, this species reportedly went extinct 50,000 years ago; some researchers believe that Bigfoot may be this species

HOMINID   Any type of human primate, both living and extinct

ICHNOLOGY   The study of footprints

NEANDERTHAL   A race of early humans from the Paleolithic Era, now believed to be extinct

OMNIVORE   A creature that consumes any kind of food, including both animal and vegetable matter

PRIMATES   The most highly developed order of mammals, including humans, apes, and monkeys

SASQUATCH   See Bigfoot

SCATOLOGY   The study of fecal samples

TRICHOLOGY   Also trichinology; the study of hair

VOCALIZATIONS   Growls, roars, hoots, screams, whistles and other sounds allegedly produced by Sasquatch, Yeti, and other ape-men

YETI   A hairy, man-like creature seen mostly in the Himalayan mountain ranges of Tibet, Nepal, China, and Russia

Endnotes

CHAPTER 1

1. Ivan T. Sanderson, *Abominable Snowmen: Legend Come to Life.* (Kempton, Ill.: Adventures Unlimited Press, 1961, 2006), 8–11, 260.

CHAPTER 2

1. Peter Byrne, *The Search for Bigfoot: Monster, Myth or Man?* (New York: Pocket Books, 1975), 15; Bernard Heuvelmans, *On the Track of Unknown Animals* (New York: Hill and Wang, Inc., 1959), 127.

2. Preston Dennett, *Supernatural California.* (Atglen, Penn.: Schiffer Books, 2006), 36–37.

3. Sanderson, 34–41.

4. John Green, *Sasquatch: The Apes Among Us* (Blaine, Wash.: Hancock House Publishers, 1978), 59; Sanderson, 67–69, 117.

CHAPTER 3

1. Loren Coleman, *Bigfoot! The True Story of Apes in America* (New York: Paraview Pocket Books, 2003), 66–70; Jeff Meldrum, *Sasquatch: Legend Meets Science* (New York: Tom Doherty Associates, LLC., 2006), 55–64.

2. Byrne, 119–128; Coleman, 81–110.

3. Green, 162–170; Grover S. Krantz, *Bigfoot Sasquatch Evidence* (Blaine, Wash.: Hancock House Publishers,

1999), 43–54, 165; John Napier, *Bigfoot, the Yeti and Sasquatch in Myth and Reality* (New York: E. P. Dutton & Co., Inc., 1973), 124.

CHAPTER 4

1. Green, 248–249.

2. Green, 189–191; Marian T. Place, *Bigfoot All Over The Country* (New York: Dodd, Mead & Company, 1978), 132–134.

3. Green, 195; Place, 130–132.

4. Janet and Colin Bord, *Bigfoot Casebook Updated: Sightings and Encounters from 1818 to 2004* (Enumclaw, Wash.: Pinewinds Press, 2006), 202–203; Green, 272–273; Philip L. Rife, *Bigfoot Across America* (Lincoln, Neb.: Writers Club Press, 2000), 61–67.

5. Robert Michael Pyle, *Where Bigfoot Walks: Crossing the Dark Divide* (New York: Houghton Mifflin Company, 1995), 275–290; Rife, 47.

CHAPTER 5

1. Carroll C. Calkins, ed., *Mysteries of the Unexplained* (Pleasantville, N.Y.: Reader's Digest Association, Inc., 1982), 163–164; Meldrum, 39–41; Napier, 53; Slavomir Rawicz, *The Long Walk: The True Story of A Trek to Freedom* (New York: Lyons & Buford Publishers, 1956), 223–232.

2. Napier, 68–69; Sanderson, 292–299; Odette Tchernine, *The Yeti* (London: Neville Spearman, 1970), 18–21, 104–105.

3. Calkins, 157–164; Krantz, 206; Tchernine, 86–87.

4. Sanderson, 158–160.

5. Ibid, 164–165.

6. Ibid, 165–166, 175–181.

7. Ibid, 189–191.

8. Calkins, 154.

CHAPTER 6

1. Meldrum, 87; Place, 86.

2. Krantz, 19.

3. Ibid, 42.

4. Krantz, 49–51, 68–69; Meldrum, 109–110.

5. Meldrum, 111–122.

6. Bord, 148; Krantz, 126–127, 207–208.

7. *Monster Quest*, "Bigfoot," aired on History Channel, November 28, 2007.

CHAPTER 7

1. Byrne, 1–4; Coleman, 193–194; Sanderson, 30, 52–57.

2. Bord, 23–24, 27–28; Rife, 71.

3. Sanderson, 4–6, 25–29, 261.

4. Interview with author in March 2005.

5. Lunetta Woods, *Story in the Snow: Bigfoot in Wisconsin* (Lakeville, Minn.: Galde Press, Inc., 1997), 4–24, 59–72.

6. Coleman, 170–177; Interview with author in January 1992.

CHAPTER 8

1. Place, 16–28.

2. Ibid, 64.

3. Krantz, 126–127.

4. Ibid., 138–139.

5. Napier, 58–59.

6. Place, 28.

Further Resources

BOOKS

Bord, Janet and Colin Bord. *Bigfoot Casebook Updated: Sightings and Encounters from 1818 to 2004.* Enumclaw, Wash.: Pinewinds Press, 2006.

Coleman, Loren. *Bigfoot! The True Story of Apes in America.* New York: Paraview Pocket Books, 2003.

Meldrum, Jeff. *Sasquatch: Legend Meets Science.* New York: Tom Doherty Associates, LLC., 2006.

Sanderson, Ivan T. *Abominable Snowmen: Legend Come to Life.* Kempton, Ill.: Adventures Unlimited Press, 1961, 2006.

WEB SITES

Bigfoot Encounters
http://www.bigfootencounters.com
This Web site is devoted to providing information about Bigfoot, and
    includes links to many other online sites.

Bigfoot Field Researchers Organization (BFRO)
http://www.bfro.net
This is the official Web site for BFRO, which is one of the leading
    civilian research organizations.

International Bigfoot Society (IBS)
http://www.internationalbigfootsociety.com
This is the official site for the IBS, which is dedicated to the study of
Bigfoot and educating the public. Lists more than 50 links to other
sites.

Oregon Bigfoot.com
http://www.oregonbigfoot.com
This site is devoted to Bigfoot encounters that have taken place in the
state of Oregon.

Texas Bigfoot Research Conservancy
http://www.texasbigfoot.com
This site is devoted to Bigfoot encounters that have taken place in the
state of Texas.

ORGANIZATIONS

UFO/Forteana Newsclipping Service
Editors: Roderick Dyke and Chuck Flood
PO Box 10950
Bainbridge Island, WA 98110
   This clipping service provides subscribers with reprints of current
newspaper articles about Bigfoot and other cryptozoological creatures.
Write for more information.

Bibliography

Bord, Janet and Colin Bord. *Bigfoot Casebook Updated: Sightings and Encounters from 1818 to 2004.* Enumclaw, Wash.: Pinewinds Press, 2006.

Byrne, Peter. *The Search for Bigfoot: Monster, Myth or Man?* New York: Pocket Books, 1975.

Calkins, Carroll C. (Editor). *Mysteries of the Unexplained.* Pleasantville, N.Y.: Reader's Digest Association, Inc., 1982.

Coleman, Loren. *Bigfoot! The True Story of Apes in America.* New York: Paraview Pocket Books, 2003.

Dennett, Preston. *Supernatural California.* Atglen, Penn.: Schiffer Books, 2006.

Grant, John. *Monster Mysteries.* Secaucus, N.J.: Chartwell Books, Inc., 1992.

Green, John. *Sasquatch: The Apes Among Us.* Blaine, Wash.: Hancock House Publishers, 1978.

Heuvelmans, Bernard. *On the Track of Unknown Animals.* New York: Hill and Wang, Inc., 1959.

Krantz, Dr. Grover S. *Bigfoot Sasquatch Evidence.* Blaine, Wash.: Hancock House Publishers, 1999.

Meldrum, Jeff. *Sasquatch: Legend Meets Science.* New York: Tom Doherty Associates, LLC., 2006.

Napier, John. *Bigfoot, the Yeti and Sasquatch in Myth and Reality.* New York: E. P. Dutton & Co., Inc., 1973.

Newton, Michael. *Strange Indiana Monsters.* Atglen, Penn.: Schiffer Publishing, 2006.

Place, Marian T. *Bigfoot All Over The Country.* New York: Dodd, Mead & Company, 1978.

Pyle, Robert Michael. *Where Bigfoot Walks: Crossing the Dark Divide.* New York: Houghton Mifflin Company, 1995.

Rawicz, Slavomir. *The Long Walk: The True Story of A Trek to Freedom*. New York: Lyons & Buford, Publishers, 1956.

Rife, Philip L. *Bigfoot Across America*. Lincoln, Neb.: Writers Club Press, 2000.

Sanderson, Ivan T. *Abominable Snowmen: Legend Come to Life*. Kempton, Ill.: Adventures Unlimited Press, 1961, 2006.

Tchernine, Odette. *The Yeti*. London: Neville Spearman, 1970.

Thorne, Ian. *Bigfoot*. Mankato, Minn.: Crestwood House, Inc., 1978.

Woods, Lunetta. *Story in the Snow: Bigfoot in Wisconsin*. Lakeville, Minn.: Galde Press, Inc., 1997.

Index

Page numbers in *italics* indicate illustrations.

About the Author

PRESTON DENNETT began investigating UFOs and the paranormal in 1986 when he discovered that his family, friends, and coworkers were having dramatic encounters. He is a field investigator for the Mutual UFO Network (MUFON) and a member of the Center for UFO Studies (CUFOS). He has investigated UFO encounters of virtually every type, and has been referred cases by the local police. He has interviewed several leading Bigfoot researchers and dozens of Bigfoot witnesses. He has written 13 books and more than 100 articles, with translations into German, Portuguese, Chinese, and Icelandic. He has appeared on numerous television and radio programs. His research has been featured in leading magazines including *Fate*, the *MUFON Journal*, and *UFO Magazine*, and in newspapers such as the *LA Times*, the *LA Daily News*, and the *Dallas Morning News*. He has taught classes about UFOs and lectures across the United States. He currently lives in Canoga Park, California. His Web site is http://www.prestondennett.com.

About the Consulting Editor

ROSEMARY ELLEN GUILEY is one of the foremost authorities on the paranormal. Psychic experiences in childhood led to her lifelong study and research of paranormal mysteries. A journalist by training, she has worked full time in the paranormal since 1983, as an author, presenter, and investigator. She has written 31 nonfiction books on paranormal topics, translated into 13 languages, and hundreds of articles. She has experienced many of the phenomena she has researched. She has appeared on numerous television, documentary, and radio shows. She is also a member of the League of Paranormal Gentlemen for Spooked Productions, a columnist for *TAPS Paramagazine*, a consulting editor for *FATE* magazine, and writer for the "Paranormal Insider" blog. Ms. Guiley's books include *The Encyclopedia of Angels*, *The Encyclopedia of Magic and Alchemy*, *The Encyclopedia of Saints*, *The Encyclopedia of Vampires, Werewolves, and Other Monsters*, and *The Encyclopedia of Witches and Witchcraft*, all from Facts On File. She lives in Maryland and her Web site is http://www.visionaryliving.com.